RUDE AWAKENINGS
FROM SLEEPING ROUGH

PETER C. MITCHELL

Stark Publishing

STARK
PUBLISHING

Rude Awakenings from Sleeping Rough / Mitchell, Peter C.
December 2020

Print ISBN: 978-1-989351-37-6
eBook ISBN: 978-1-989351-38-3

As the author of this work I do not authorize its use in whole or in part for any charity fund-raising or awareness raising campaigns. - Peter C. Mitchell

FOR JENNY,

THE HARDER THE JOURNEY
THE SWEETER THE SUCCESS

TABLE OF CONTENTS

Preface

I woke up in St. James Park this morning to find a man masturbating over me while I slept.

Bizarrely, my first reaction was "Thank God it's not a cop." The harsh reality of what I had woken to quickly became evident; but by that point the pervert had tucked himself back into his track-pants and was running away.

The incident didn't end there.

Realizing my day was starting at 3:50 a.m. I gathered myself together and was disgusted to find the top of my jeans and bottom of my shirt were damp with his pre-ejaculation discharge. The smell was easily masked with the aerosol deodorant in my rucksack, but the dampness and discomfort that came with it would have to wait for the sun to rise.

As I headed out of the park, I stopped at a rubbish bin to roll a cigarette. The pervert came out of nowhere to tell me to be careful because somebody had been wanking over me while I was sleeping, then scurried off again. He then turned around and started walking back to me, exposed penis in hand, pleasuring himself furiously and asking me if I liked it.

I was alarmed but not frightened. This wasn't the first disturbing incident I've faced since I found myself in the streets of London, and likely won't be the last. I have received self-defence lessons from friends in the homeless community and can defend myself enough to buy time and run from a situation.

I grabbed my keys from my pocket and made a fist, slipping them between my fingers, ready to punch him in the eye if necessary. I swung my arm threateningly, shouting at him to "Get the fuck away from me now!" It was enough. He ran away again. He followed at a distance for a brief time, but once I was out of the park and on the street, he disappeared into the darkness and I didn't see him again.

Please Allow Me to Introduce Myself

My name is Peter Mitchell. Peter Christian Mitchell to be precise, for reasons that will soon become chillingly evident. My entry into this world was about as inauspicious as entries get. My parents had met while working at the BBC, fallen in love –as parents do– and married, when they quickly and lovingly engaged in the parental duties of starting a family. I was the first of two by-products of those parental duties, arriving on 16 March 1968 in Princess Louise Hospital in the Kensington district of London, a relatively nice place to enter the world.

In October of that year we emigrated to Canada and eventually settled in Hamilton, Ontario where my father climbed the ink-stained media ladder to become an award-winning Business Editor for the Hamilton Spectator. My mother, when she wasn't being unceremoniously dragged into the daily dramatics provided by my younger sister and myself, also eked out a successful career in freelance journalism in a wide range of areas. Our den was filled to bursting with files and photos relating to mercenaries, wrestlers, Jack the Ripper, and the paranormal. Scooby-Doo was educational programming in our household. "There are no such things as ghosts; only people trying to make money," was a lesson learned at the same time Big Bird was teaching the ABC's. My mother's most notable accomplishment was uncovering the all-too-human machinations behind the spectral apparitions of Borley Rectory, known for decades as "The Most Haunted House in England." Forty years later the members of the Borley Tourism Committee still haven't forgiven her.

Rest in peace Mum.

Ghostbusting aside, it was a fairly normal, non-descript, stereotypically bland Canadian childhood. My teenage self may disagree, but it was relatively free of the drama and trauma that teenagers love to wallow in. Friends moved away. Pets died. I had surgery on an ingrown toenail. I failed my Driver's Examination on my first attempt. And my second. I sometimes wonder if I only passed on my third effort because the instructor feared the possibility of getting into a moving vehicle with me ever again. It was hardly "Catcher in the Rye" material; just the typical journey through the standard rites of passage we all pass through as we enter the great global tribe of Humanity.

I reached adulthood, joined the tribe, and worked my way through University to earn a Bachelor of Arts degree in English Literature; essentially spending four years and thousands of my father's dollars proving to the world I could read. Big Bird had done his job well, free of charge.

I eventually followed in my father's footsteps, bumbling my way through a moderately successful career in business journalism. Though I served as Editor for two local business magazines for a few years, there were no awards coming my way. It wasn't quite my cup of tea and I was merely treading water until my proverbial ship came in. Evidently, as we all discover, that ship has yet to leave port.

Researching an article on Corporate Social Responsibility and the philanthropic role local business leaders were playing in alleviating social issues caught my interest. It prompted me to start exploring a long-forgotten philanthropist in our family's history, Sir John Kirk. As Secretary and Director of the Ragged School Union, John championed the rights of children, the disabled, and the working poor in Victorian London. My early research indicated his influence extended far beyond London's city limits, and his life proved far more interesting than previous biographies revealed. I had even discovered an obscure link between my illustrious ancestor and Jack the Ripper that had escaped the notice of the most ardent *Ripperologists* –including my mother.

Inspired by this and other salacious family revelations, I dove head-first into the writing of "A Knight in the Slums," a self-confessed Sanity/Vanity project that quickly took over my life and ultimately lured me down the path to self-destruction. Call it ego; call it a midlife crisis; call it what you will, I pursued this dream project with a passion and foolhardiness that saw the dream eventually descend into nightmare.

In early 2017 my fiftieth birthday was looming uncomfortably on the horizon, teasing me with the absence of any substantial accomplishments in a half-century of living. My father had won awards. My mother had unravelled the spectral shenanigans of England's Most Haunted House. Sir John had achieved world-wide respect and accolades for his work among the destitute. Even my grandfather, Frank Mitchell, had earned an O.B.E. for his work as the Press and Information Officer for the British Embassy in Washington, D.C. (annoying the Beatles in the process). I hadn't even raised a cactus with any degree of success, and with the big 5-0 staring me in the face it was weighing heavily.

"A Knight in the Slums" was my mid-life sports car; my one chance to leave some kind of legacy to the world so I wouldn't be forgotten in the years after I departed it. To complete the research, I had to return to those same London slums John Kirk once walked. So that is just what I did, with the minimum of preparation, blinded by the light of my dream.

I did have a precedent from my own distant past I was using as a template. I had moved to England in 1999 for a period of two years with practically no groundwork laid ahead of time. I had been able to find accommodation and employment with relative ease and was firmly established within a matter of weeks. It worked then, I reasoned, there was no reason it shouldn't work again. But I was much older now. England was older now. And as I would soon discover, England today shares more in common with the England of Sir John's youth than with mine.

On 16 March 2017 –my 49th birthday– I called the British Government to obtain my National Insurance Number from previous employment records. I was informed that information could not be provided over the phone. That was reasonable enough, so I asked if she would mind pulling my file to see if there were any potential issues I should know about. She happily agreed and after a few moments replied, "Oh yeah; here you are. No problems." She cheerily wished me a safe voyage and disconnected, eager to take her next call.

She had lied.

She had not called up my file at all, for as it later transpired, there was no file to retrieve. It wasn't the first bald-faced lie I had been told by an employee of Her Majesty's Civil Service, and it likely won't be the last; but it was the innocent lie on which all future events hinged. Had I known ahead of time the problems that were about to emerge I would never have booked my flight.

I arrived in London 28 May 2017, settled into the Travel Hostel I had booked, purchased a mobile phone and a lap-top, and started putting the wheels in motion to start the exciting new voyage before me with a "King of the World" confidence that proved more hubristically prophetic than anyone could have guessed.

Some time passed before a slightly disturbing thought crept into my mind: the wheels weren't moving. After days of phone calls and emails I finally discovered why.

The government had no proof I existed.

The reason eventually given was the hospital where I had been born –the Princess Louise— had closed, and the records had been lost. It did not explain how I was able to obtain my passport three years previously, but the response to that query was stone cold silence.

There was one more little complication that proved the iceberg to my Titanic. The government seemingly had no proof *I* existed, but it had ample proof of the existence of *another* Peter Mitchell. A Sex Offender. The worst kind of Sex Offender: a paedophile. The little digital nanobots in Her Royal Majesty's computer systems put two and two together and came up with five. The result: I now had pride of place on the Sex Offender Registry.

Wherever he may be in that Great Beyond, the ghost of George Orwell snorted coffee through his nose at that little twist of bureaucratic fate.

One of the many perks in being classified a Sex Offender is your placement on the No-Fly List. (Those little digital nanobots are nothing if not efficient, even when their math doesn't add up.) Barring a long swim, I couldn't return to Canada. I contacted the Canadian High Commission on Trafalgar Square, and discovered to my horror that I had not just become a victim of my own mid-life ego, but of my nonchalant apathy towards the life I had been living across the Atlantic.

Though I had lived in Canada for the majority of my 49 years, I had never obtained Canadian citizenship. I saw no need. It was costly, time-consuming, and had only affected my ability to vote –not something I considered a high priority as I cynically felt my one little vote didn't make any difference at all in the Greater Scheme of Things. It turns out the Greater Scheme meets indifference with indifference. The Canadian High Commission couldn't help me because I wasn't a Canadian Citizen. End of story. The nice gentleman on the phone wished me luck and disconnected, eager to take his next call.

Fortunately, I still had my original birth certificate, my recent passport, my Canadian Driver's Licence and, of all things, my Burlington Public Library card to prove to the powers that be that:

A) The person sitting in front of them did exist despite the assertions of their databases to the contrary; and

B) The records of every book, DVD, Blue-Ray, CD, and magazine I had ever borrowed from the Burlington Public Library ultimately proving I was not in England at the time of the offences. It seems the only way to survive in our Brave New World is to fight databases with databases. It was touch and go for a while, but the Burlington Public Library database emerged victorious. Halleluiah.

While this mess was being sorted, I rented temporary accommodation in the Bayswater area, just a five-minute walk from the flat my parents were renting when I was born. I explored the area extensively, sharing photos with my father back in Canada while he shared the memories they inspired. I put the job-search on the backburner and spent weeks in the British Library taking photographs of the hundreds of documents they possessed relating to John Kirk and his work for later transcription. I also emptied my meagre savings and began paying for rent and basic living expenses with my Canadian credit card. I had no choice at the time. The matter was resolved quite quickly, but when the option to return to Canada briefly became available, I fell victim to my third liability: pigheaded stubbornness.

I could have returned. In hindsight I should have returned. Friends and family had generously offered to help with the flight, resettlement, and rebuilding. But I didn't take advantage of the opportunity to go back. Before arriving in England, I had spent over five years gathering research and making preliminary notes for "A Knight in the Slums." I had thousands of pages of documentation but needed more. Returning to Canada would force me to discard the project for good and my only legacy would be an aborted attempt at my magnum opus, abandoned at the first hurdle.

I reasoned, not entirely without merit, that I had simply had a run of bad luck that had amounted to nothing more than a detour on the path to success. That luck had surely changed and turning back now would be turning my back on the opportunities I was finally free to pursue. I would spend the rest of my life filled with regret, wondering what could have been.

And truth be told I was annoyed at Canada. I felt, rightly or wrongly, that the country I had contributed to for 49 years had cavalierly turned its back on me in my hour of need over a piece of paper. I was a mere "Permanent Resident" as opposed to a "Canadian Citizen", and in my state of mind at the time that distinction meant my contributions to the country meant nothing; that my life had meant nothing. I was in no hurry to return with my tail between my legs.

So I stayed. Foolishly, I stayed. Employment remained stubbornly out of reach, but I kept calm. My available credit shrank, yet I carried on; my debt rising to frightening levels. I eventually surpassed my limit and my card was cancelled. The inevitable outcome had not just appeared over the horizon, it was barrelling towards me with frightening speed. I could see it; I could hear it; I could smell the disaster about to claim me, but I couldn't believe it was happening. I faced the catastrophe head-on, not from any sense of courage, but from a numbing sense of disbelief. Disaster struck and life, as I had known it, changed forever.

Ego.

Apathy.

Obstinacy.

Denial.

Play those cards right and you can be elected a leader of the free world. Play them wrong and, well . . .

. . . that's how I, a self-confessed middle-class twit from Canada, wound up homeless on the streets of London.

And that was only the beginning . . .

Down and Out in London

An earlier version of this testimony was performed as the finale for "Down and Out Live," staged in London on 6 June 2018, and in Paris on 28 September 2018.

It was also published in the Huffington Post on 6 June 2018.

For years you have passed them on the streets, as much a part of your routine as your morning shower, your half-hearted scan of the world's news —fake or otherwise— and the barista who artistically crafts the £4 cappuccino with soya milk, three drops of vanilla, and a flutter of chocolate sprinkles that has to be made just right or it throws your day off in ways that nobody else understands.

You see them as often as you see your own family. The disenfranchised. The rough sleepers. The homeless. Camped out and befouling the sidewalks and alleyways of your daily commute, their worldly possessions, such as they are, spread around them —as dirty and worn out as the sleepers themselves, but as valuable to them as your £100 brogues are to you.

Occasionally you get the urge to throw some loose change at them as a gesture of magnanimous humanity, but when push comes to shove you would rather tip the honest, hard-working barista who ensures your day gets off to a proper start. Better to support the successful rather than throw good money after bad trying to keep the great unwashed afloat.

You have conditioned yourself to look through them –allowing your eyes to pass over them without actually seeing them. A defeated acceptance of lives gone wrong; uncomfortable reminders of what can happen when the best laid plans of mice and men go horribly awry. "Thank god I'm not like them," you think, sipping your £4 cup of liquid gold. "I could never let that happen to me."

Until suddenly –inexplicably– it does. And you discover the life you have built was nothing more than a house of cards that crashed down around you with frightening ease. A spate of bad luck, a poor decision or two, and the ubiquitous 'circumstances beyond your control' conspire to create a perfect storm of events that leaves you cast away on the streets feeling dazed, disjointed, and damned.

"This is wrong," you think. "I'm not like them."

You don't sleep the first night, nor the second. You wander aimlessly –a rucksack over your shoulder and a suitcase trundling behind you. Your remaining worldly possessions –a few shirts, socks, underwear, and toiletries– as valuable to you now as your £100 brogues were mere days before.

Your mind, unable to process the enormity of your new world order, shuts down. Time crawls to the rhythm of your slow shuffle. You pass through your surroundings with the same unseeing stare you once reserved only for your fellow rough sleepers. You are unable to say where you've been; where you're going; or what you are doing. You no longer lay claim to the right of moving from Point A to Point B. Your journey has no point. Your life no longer has a point.

As reality gains an ugly foothold, denial kicks into overdrive. This isn't really happening. It's a mistake. A hiccup. A very bad dream. Click your heels and chant, "There's no place like home," and all will be right with the world again.

But there are no wizards in the real world – you no longer have a home. Yet the fantasy of denial continues to entice with each stubborn wave of its magic wand . . .

. . . until physical reality creeps in and breaks it.

Your body does its best to adapt to your new circumstances but fights a losing battle. Your sleep pattern changes – slipping away from the doctor approved eight hours per night to a restless series of two-hour micronaps scattered across a 24-hour cycle.

You make a valiant effort to stay clean and presentable, but it too proves a battle you are destined to lose. You master the unique and time consuming art of public toilet bathing; hiding in a stall in your underwear waiting for the facilities to clear, then dashing to the sinks for a splash of water and squirt of soap, then dashing back to the stall to wash one body part at a time. Invariably, someone catches you mid-dash and you wince at the look of sheer contempt they throw in your direction. It is a look you grow to know well.

Despite your efforts, toilet bathing is a poor substitute for showering in the comfort of your own home. You grow increasingly unkempt; your clothes start to smell "well-worn"; and your skin begins to itch –a foreshadowing of the rashes that will soon follow.

Your limbs start to ache from the burden of endlessly wandering with your life hanging off your back. Your shoulders stiffen. Your legs seize up. Your knees become hubs of throbbing pain. And your feet –dear god your feet– nothing in life prepares you for the hell your feet inflict on you.

Your soles grow tender from the never-ending pounding of the pavement. Callouses form, then split, leaving ridges of sharp agony that sting with every step. Blisters develop and burst. Your toes, confined to such tight quarters for such an unnatural length of time, begin to itch. And burn. The skin between them softens, then splits, adding the moisture of blood and pus to the itching, burning mess.

"It can't get any worse," you promise yourself.

The promise breaks. It gets worse.

One of the wheels on your suitcase breaks, and you discover just what it means to be a slave to your possessions –your only possessions– the pathetic final reminders of your once perfect life. Your overtaxed body is forced to add the weight of the suitcase to its already painful burden. You switch hands frequently, but both arms quickly succumb to the dead weight of your life dragging them down. The callouses that plague your feet spread to your palms with the same devastating effects. Your world shrinks even further as you are forced to confine your activities –such as they are– to one small area because the pain of movement becomes too great to bear.

The nights grow colder. Your body, weakened by lack of sleep, lack of nutrition, and lack of comfort, develops a deep, set-in-your-bones chill that even the warmth of day can't erase. You are assaulted by random bouts of shivering that attack without warning, day and night. Your mind begins to flirt with the darkest of thoughts, contemplating the final option that would guarantee an end to your misery. But still, somehow, you solider on.

Then the final –unthinkable– horror strikes. In the wee dark hours of the morning you are woken by the call of nature –demanding more than the usual urinary sacrifice. The luxury of a common toilet is denied you as the public conveniences are inconveniently closed until the first light of day. You pray with a conviction never felt before that you can wait it out. But nature will not be denied. Discomfort turns to pain, and you realise there is only one humiliating option available.

You scan your immediate surroundings for a discrete make-shift lavatory. Nature itself provides the solution with dark irony, and you select a clump of bushes that will provide the minimum of privacy. Zombie-like, you make your way to the place of ultimate humiliation, furtively scanning the sidewalks and roadways for any unwanted passers-by. You slowly take your position, and with a self-loathing you have never before known, void your bowels like a common animal –the most basic of bodily functions regressing you to your most bestial nature.

You make your way back to the bench that serves as your bed with the indignity of your actions fresh in your mind. Your body aches. Your feet itch, burn, sting. A fresh wave of shivering strikes. You shake uncontrollably. Your teeth chatter. Finally, you break. Tears explode from your eyes, mixing with the phlegm that streams through your nose. Your breath heaves in deep wailing gasps. There are no wizards in the real world –you no longer have a home.

"This is wrong," you splutter. "I'm not like them."

"I'm not that strong."

Somehow you survive the night. You find yourself hovering around one of the city shelters set up to help those the city has rejected; your preconceived notions preventing you from taking that final step.

"I'm going to be robbed, drugged, and sodomised," you argue. "While the staff hold hands in a sharing circle quoting Bible verses and singing 'Kumbaya'; oblivious to the scum and villainy that surrounds them. I'm better off on the streets. I'm not like them."

Then a fresh wave of shivering starts and you find yourself crossing the threshold, wanting nothing more than a few scant moments of warmth. The warmth you receive is not the warmth you were expecting, and you find yourself momentarily surprised. As the staff listen to the story of your fall, you scan their eyes for a hint of judgment, but search in vain. Their eyes remain expressionless and their smiles frozen as they take copious notes relating to your fall. But the biggest surprise is yet to come.

Your fellow occupants admit you into their ranks without question. The very people you once dehumanised as generic 'Homeless' see the human in you. They offer a hand of acceptance you haltingly, hypocritically take because you are still not quite prepared to grant the same in return. Until, despite yourself, you start to see the human in them.

The earth mother that shines through the wreckage of drug addiction, one of the first to welcome you and make you feel comfortable. She makes sure everyone gets their fair share when volunteers pass through bringing warm meals and clothing.

The father figure that surfaces through the haze of chronic alcoholism –forbidden from contact with his own children, yet willing to share his parental wisdom– offering support, practical advice, and a guiding hand to those newly fallen into this strange new world.

The military veteran, scarred by the mental and emotional wounds of seeing things no one should ever see in the field of battle, who takes a protective view of his new "troop" and is the first to come to the defence of the weak and the bullied.

For you have fallen into the only truly inclusive group of people in the history of civilisation. The story of everyone's fall is unique and cannot be brushed away with dehumanising labels. There is no segregation; no discrimination; no distinction based on race, religion, skin colour, gender, sexuality, or age. Everyone is welcome to fall; and many do. Homelessness is the great equaliser, with many entrances but few exits.

Sadly, too many focus on the causes of the fall, and not the solutions needed to help the fallen regain their footing. They become clients, cases, numbers, ticked boxes, statistics. The person behind the statistics gets mislaid in "the process".

If you truly want to understand that rough sleeper befouling the sidewalk in front of your favourite coffee shop; the answer is simple.

Ask their name.

Remind them they are a human being.

Just ask their name.

My name is Peter. Peter Christian Mitchell to be precise. I am happy to share my name with anyone who asks.

To Sleep: Perchance to Dream

It has been said in space no-one can hear you scream. On Planet Earth the screams surround us but go un-heard. They simply add to the general cacophony of modern life. The crashing and thumping of roadwork and construction; the screeching of music indoors and out; one-sided phone conversations passing by; fights erupting; tires squealing; horns blaring; sirens wailing; babies crying; dogs barking. . .. The screams of the home-less simply add to the ruckus and get lost in the aural haze.

Everybody sees the homeless; several study them; but few truly listen to them. People, whether their intentions are noble or narcistic, add to the din with their self-anointed missions to "raise awareness". Individual social justice warriors roam the streets, snapping photographs to share on social media with links to articles detailing the suffering and abuse of rough sleepers without verifying if the stories are current or true, or if the rough sleepers actually want their pictures taken and their suffering shared. Charity think tanks "gather information" –the same information they have been gathering for decades–and present reports –the same reports they have been presenting for decades– that invariably blame the government and the parents –and demand more money to fight these twin "evils." Politicians periodically wander their constituencies 'spontaneously' visiting shelters that have had days to prepare and taking impromptu selfies with 'charity-selected' representatives of the derelict community. And they all publicly congratulate themselves for giving the homeless a voice.

With all due respect to the noble, it's crap.

Pure self-aggrandizing crap.

They are bringing awareness to a problem everyone already knows exists. People see it every day. Nobody wants repetitive "awareness"; they want fresh solutions. Those solutions currently in place, many initiated by John Kirk and other philanthropists in the late 19th Century, are simply not working. They are porous with corruption and abuse, and do not reflect the reality of life on the streets today. Bringing awareness to an already visible problem helps raise funds but does not actually help the rough sleepers achieve any sustainable stability. It hasn't for almost 200 years.

It simply adds to the noise.

And the homeless are perfectly capable of speaking for themselves thank you very much. They don't need charity 'filters' to make them more palatable, more cuddly, more 'marketable'. They don't appreciate their stories being conveniently 'edited' to fit pre-defined categories that may not necessarily reflect the truth of their circumstances. They are more than capable of telling their stories themselves, warts and all, so the general public can learn just how dreadful their existence is, and just how inadequate the current solutions are. The homeless are decidedly not cuddly, and that is why their true voices need to be heard.

For the streets are vicious. You have to be tough to endure. I have seen a man tasered by police in Charing Cross when a simple disagreement turned violent and bloody. I have watched medical personnel attend to the thrashing, screaming, foaming-at-the-mouth body of a man suffering a drug overdose in Trafalgar Square. I have tended to the cuts and bruises of a colleague beaten by a group of 'respectable' middle class lads out for a drunken night on the town. I have learned how to dodge a punch, and more disturbingly, how to throw one. At the age of fifty-one I struck another man for the first time in self-defense. Some nights I lie in bed and still feel the red dew of his blood on my fist.

This is the reality. This is life on the streets. This is the struggle above and beyond mere food and shelter that the homeless face every day. They need a permanent, sustainable escape route. They need a break from the battle; they need a break from the elements; they need a break from the crap. More often than not they have no choice but to settle for a temporary reprieve. Even if only for one night.

Night shelters provide a place to sleep; but not necessarily a place to sleep well. The unfamiliar surroundings;

the strobe-light effect of dozens of strange faces moving around you; and the underlying uncertainty of what tomorrow will bring conspire to prevent you from falling into the deep sleep your mind and body so desperately crave. You eat your meal if one is provided; you claim your cot if one is provided; you hunker down, shut your eyes, and do your best to catch 40 winks in an unfamiliar room surrounded by strangers.

Just as the bliss of slumber is seconds away you find yourself jolted awake by the cruelest of truths. You can escape the cold; you can escape the rain; you can escape the hunger; but you can never escape the snoring. Dante himself would add an Eighth Circle of Hell to his repertoire if he experienced the symphony of snores that performs –free of charge– every night in city shelters. It starts with a single solitary snore, piercing the darkness and establishing the rhythm for other nasal instruments to follow. It is soon joined by another –higher in pitch and longer in duration– their ear-shattering duet weaving together in horribly imperfect harmony. They are joined by a third. Then a fourth. A fifth. Like Ravel's Bolero the repetitive tune continues to swell as more performers add their nocturnal acoustics to the music of the night. Then the mutterings begin –the exaggerated sighs –the growls –the increasingly colourful cursing serving as counterpoint –all rising together to an ear-splitting crescendo punctuated by the roar of "Shurrup!" and the thunk and clatter of cots being violently kicked. The orchestra is silenced for a few brief moments. Then it all starts again, a Sisyphean cycle of auditory torment.

This is followed in the morning by the even more absurd theatrics of 30 or more men vying for the three sinks, four shower stalls, and three toilets in a room barely large enough to swing the proverbial cat as they attempt their morning ablutions. It is a surreal ballet performed by street-scarred, life-hardened, smelly, hairy men –damp towels serving as tutus; crusty socks as slippers– weaving and bobbing, shoving and jostling, cursing and gesturing in a morbidly choreographed celebration of male hygiene. Swan Lake it ain't.

But somehow it works. Homelessness makes stranger bedfellows than politics, and the strongest friendships are forged in the grimmest circumstances. You quickly grow accustomed to the faces around you. Despite your initial hesitation you forge bonds, make acquaintances, and establish friendships with men you would not have granted a second glance before you found yourself among them. You share your stories –horrific and humorous– of life on the streets. You trade tips, advice, and practical solutions to the personal hygiene problems that invariably flare up. There's no room for the shy or the precious: you discuss hemorrhoids with the same breezy nonchalance as you do the weather, especially when they tear –a horrifying occurrence the first time it happens, but one that becomes as regular as the seasons.

Shoulders to cry on are available in those moments it overwhelms you, and tissues, generally nicked from the local shop, are freely offered to wipe your nose when the tears subside. Sweaters, blankets, towels –anything that provides some semblance of warmth– are traded back and forth depending on whose need is greater. Twenty pence –in the context of street life, 20 pence can some days be as life changing as a million pounds– 20 pence is often freely handed from one friend to another to ensure he eats or, in all honesty, drinks that day. Whether you are an alcoholic, a drug addict, an ex-convict, or a middle-class twit, you need those friendships if you want to survive in the streets.

Unfortunately, not all friends are chosen wisely.

All the World's A Stage

I had arrived in London the final week of May 2017. By the final week of April 2018, I was cast adrift in the streets. Eleven months was the fleeting length of time it took for a dream to descend into nightmare. Eleven months for the inconceivable to become reality. Eleven months to slide headlong into ruin. Eleven short months.

I was down. I was dirty. I was cold and damp. But I wasn't quite as out as Orwell had surmised. I knew from my own research mechanisms were in place to deal with exactly this type of situation; that my own ancestor had helped put the wheels in motion over 150 years ago. Perhaps Sir John himself would indirectly provide the salvation I needed from beyond the grave. It was the least he could do to show his appreciation for the years of work I had put into shining a light on his charitable labours –the same labours that would now rise up and save his wayward descendant. Even down and out, I was the same self-important middle-class twit I was before my fall.

I contacted Crisis, Shelter, St. Mungo's, and other charities via email to explain my situation and ask what assistance they provided, particularly in relation to obtaining employment. Despite being on the streets, housing was not a concern as I had left on good terms with my former landlord and could easily return. I simply needed assistance finding work so I could pay the rent. Over the space of two weeks I sent dozens of emails.

Not one charity responded.

Eventually another rough sleeper recognized my plight and took me to the Salvation Army office on Princes Street. They in turn passed me on to The Connection, one of multiple charities dealing with homelessness under the auspices of St. Martin-in-the-Fields Church. Dutifully making the trek I knocked on The Connection's big red door and was dutifully signed into their Day Centre. Unfortunately, I could not stay in their Night Shelter without a referral from London's "No Second Night Out" initiative. It had taken two weeks and two separate charities to get noticed, and now I had another wait for what appeared to be an unnecessary piece of bureaucracy. A long and winding road indeed, but I considered myself lucky that my journey into homelessness was coming to an end after a comparatively short time.

Except it didn't end.

Despite the logical assumption their very name provides, I did endure a second night out. And a third. In fact, I spent almost *two weeks* of additional "Nights Out" at Marble Arch where I had gotten to know the local street cleaners on a first name basis; and was grateful for the cups of coffee and dinners they had started to bring.

It took *eight* attempts at contact before one of the "No Second Night Out" Teams arrived.

Even then, my deliverance was by happenstance more than planned design. The two outreach workers had arrived to pick up another rough sleeper who had shown up that very night, and completely passed me by. Had I not taken the initiative to introduce myself, I can't help but wonder if I would still be sleeping at Marble Arch to this very day receiving nourishment and sustenance from the generous low-income night workers of Westminster during those cold, occasionally rainy nights.

In the meantime, I visited the Day Centre at The Connection, lugging my rucksack and broken suitcase back and forth between Marble Arch and Trafalgar Square on a daily basis. It was worth the effort to take advantage of the showers, laundry service, and hot lunches that were provided. Initially I was taken aback by the fees they charged for the meal. The Night Centre provided dinner for free, but those making use of the Day Centre had to pay to eat. A pittance admittedly, but when you're penniless even a pittance can be a luxury expense. Many 20 pence pieces were passed back and forth among the hungriest of the homeless.

They helped compensate for the expense with free meal tickets that were distributed to volunteers and participants in various creative and self-help initiatives; or used as rewards for those exhibiting actions that pleased their case workers. These tickets, along with the even more valuable bus tokens, were frequently traded or sold for pennies as part of the bartering economy of the disenfranchised, and often added to the financial chaos that life on the streets brings. But beggars can't be choosers. They can only accept the charges and conditions forced upon them and make do the best they can, no matter how chaotic the results.

Luckily a good friend in Toronto had lent me a sum of money once I had signed on with The Connection as we were both under the assumption that salvation was at hand. Under the conditions of my "Permanent Resident" status in Canada, I could only be out of the country for two years before that status expired and I would have to re-apply as a new immigrant. I still had slightly more than a year before I had to return, and we were both confident I would be thanking him in person before that year was complete.

It wasn't to be.

From Day One I met with a rotating team of volunteers and social workers. I was assigned an official case worker, who was promptly replaced by another, who was subsequently swapped for a third. I would later realize the "case worker" designation is a bit of a red herring. Every conversation with any staff member or volunteer –even some fellow service users– is open to scrutiny, to interpretation, and to amateur diagnosis. Smoking areas especially are hotspots for cocked ears and mental note taking. Your case worker is merely the conductor. It creates an atmosphere of paranoia that keeps service users on their toes, and on the defensive.

The more battle-hardened rough sleepers learn to casually dole out different pieces of misinformation to different people to find out what comes back to them through their case workers. It throws the amateur psychologists off whatever scent they're pursuing, and roots out the charity 'pets' who, sometimes knowingly, sometimes not, are used to gather information on their fellow street mates. Lab rats can't fight back. People can.

With naïve trust I recounted the story behind my circumstances many times to many people who dutifully took notes. I quickly picked up on the fact their side of the conversation was peppered with phrases like "You can't say that," or "What you mean to say is…", and they would make the necessary 'corrections' for their files, without ever revealing the corrections –or files– to me. It was a pattern I noticed throughout my ordeal not only in my conversations with the charities, but with the Department of Works and Pensions, the local councils and, later, the Metropolitan Police. Over time I discovered my official files did not accurately record my statements, my situation, or my consent. They simply served to classify me according to 'ticked boxes' that did not necessarily reflect my situation or apply labels that definitely did not apply. I was not being heard, merely processed.

In almost every interview and "casual chat" my tremors were addressed, understandably so. I have a vitamin deficiency, am perennially underweight, and my body fat percentage is often at risk of dropping to dangerously low levels. It is a physiology I inherited from Sir John Kirk himself. He managed to turn it to his advantage by becoming a celebrity spokesperson for "Phosferine": an opium-based cure-all tonic that was all the rage in the early 20th Century. I can barely remember to take my vitamin supplements when I can actually be bothered to purchase them, so won't be signing any endorsement contracts any time soon. The condition is genetic, the apathy my own.

One of the consequences is a slight tremor that becomes more pronounced during times of stress. It is often confused with alcohol withdrawal so I wasn't particularly surprised when the charity workers expressed concern, and gladly answered all the questions related to addiction, even the one that would later be used against me many times:

Is there a history of alcoholism in your family?

Yes.

My mother was an alcoholic. Drink was a demon that plagued her for years. It was never a 'secret'; never a 'scandal'; never as destructive a force as I would encounter amongst the alcoholic friends I made on Trafalgar Square and the 'charity approved' housing I was later forced to accept. It was simply her cross to bear and a part of the fabric of life. She did eventually conquer it –as best as alcoholics can. With no proper support from family or friends that didn't fully understand the condition or its pain, and without seeking support from organizations that offer assistance; she made the not-so-simple decision to stop drinking.

And she did. Through sheer willpower.

Before she passed away from unrelated causes years later, she often said it was the hardest thing she had ever done. It was one of her proudest accomplishments; and one she was never afforded the credit she deserved. I was a smug, snotty, know-it-all twenty-something at the time and my response was invariably a bored "Yeah Mum; whatever." It wasn't until I found myself homeless –befriended and looked after by the alcoholics whose disease had led them to the same destination– that I gained a deeper appreciation of the suffering she endured and the strength it took to overcome it. They didn't just teach me the skills to survive; they taught me empathy, humanity, and the knowledge that you will never truly understand the suffering of another unless you share that same pain. Would I have gained that insight without them? Probably not.

Sorry Mum.

That insight, however, was still months away. For now, I was simply providing the "expert" social workers with the information they required for my file so they could get the "complete picture" of the circumstances that led to my homelessness. It wasn't relevant in my opinion, but I did understand the concern surrounding my tremors and happily answered all questions with complete honesty. They had my best interests at heart, so who was I to question them? Had I known how the information would be used against me, I would never have been so forthcoming.

Besides, my main interest was finding the path that would lead me *off* the streets, not the path that led me there. I was more concerned with obtaining employment than housing as I could easily return to my previous flat once I had a guaranteed income. My goal was to start working so I could pay the rent and start making payments on my credit card before my deadline to return to Canada expired. My case worker explained The Connection could only assist if I signed up for Job Seeker's Allowance. When I indicated it wasn't necessary to claim any benefits as a friend had loaned me some money, I was informed it was the only way the charity could help. This debate continued for a few days before I capitulated, voicing my concerns over how unnecessary it was. It was duly noted.

Almost immediately I was pressured to apply for housing benefits with the same unyielding admonition that I could not receive help unless I did. I again clarified I did not need assistance finding housing as I could return to my former residence once I could guarantee the payment of rent that employment would provide. I was told I didn't understand the system, that it was too complicated to explain, and informed for the first time I had to learn to "play the game." It was an impasse that went on for weeks. This pressure to sign on for benefits I did not need would continue throughout my charity experience, and eventually take a disturbing turn.

While frustrating, the relationship was by no means fractious in those early days. I dove into their job search assistance programme with gusto; updated my computer skills; participated in their book club and mindfulness sessions –always with an eye to obtaining a meal ticket or two; and successfully completed a Health and Safety Training for Food Handling course they recommended. I did question the recommendation as it was not in any way a natural extension of the skills I had built in journalism over the past 20 years. I was "unofficially" told it helps them "keep their numbers up" and it was always advisable to "show willingness on my part". It wasn't explicitly stated but it was basically a "You scratch our back; we'll scratch yours" mentality common in the charity sector.

Help the charity, and the charity will help you.

Besides, the staff of The Connection were well aware of my existing skills and finding ways to use them within the organization. I was told of a multi-charity history club they felt would be a perfect fit, particularly in relation to my research relating to poverty and the history of the charity system. They were eager for me to use my knowledge of poverty in the Victorian Era to show how effective the charities of today were in comparison to those of the past. I was open to the idea after I was back on my feet and earning a stable income, and even suggested it as a possibility for employment within a charity. The suggestion was met with polite, stone faced smiles. Duly noted.

I also engaged in some intriguing conversations with their Impact and Evidence Coordinator (A lovely job title with a lovely salary. It looks good on the curriculum vitae.) about "Nudge Theory", a concept I remembered becoming vogue in the business community during my

journalism days. It is a method of using positive reinforcement and indirect suggestions to influence human
behaviour. It had long been abandoned by reputable
businesses for the very real ethical concerns surrounding
psychological manipulation and the potential use of negative reinforcement. The concept had now surfaced in the
charity industry and appeared to be embraced whole-
heartedly. I smugly assumed it was pursued as a method
to encourage donations from the general public. Over the
following months I realized its applications as a means to
enforce 'charity approved' decisions or force people into
making choices that were decidedly not in their best interest gave truth to the business community's ethical
concerns. However, that insight too was yet to come. For
now, it was simply a welcome intellectual conversation.

A beacon of light soon appeared. I had been continuing my job search at the local library and had obtained
temporary employment handing out an entertainment
newspaper at various train stations in London on a
weekly basis for the next month. I did have a slight hurdle to overcome. I could not easily traverse the city with
my broken suitcase in tow. My activities were limited to
Trafalgar Square from the closing of the Day Centre at
1:00 to the opening of the Night Shelter at 9:00. As many
of The Connection's service users do, I spent those eight
hours listening to the buskers at Trafalgar Square, within
sight of the red and white maple leaf flags that adorned
the Canadian High Commission, a mere stone's throw

away from The Connection. They were a daily –sometimes positive, sometimes painful– reminder of "home"; the home to which I still hoped to return.

The Connection does have lockers, but I was informed they were all in use. It is also possible to arrange to leave suitcases and belongings behind during the day based on criteria that are never clearly outlined and seemingly based on the mood and whim of the particular staff member you ask. I assumed taking paid employment would meet that criteria.

Silly me.

I asked again and received the default reply of "Too busy." I asked again. And again. And received the same automated response: "Too busy." Finally, on my fourth request, I was granted permission, but for one afternoon only. I was informed it was taking advantage of their services and told how grateful I should be it was being allowed. Though taken aback by the rudeness I chalked it up to that particular staff member having a bad day. I was too eager to get back to work, even if just for one day, to worry about it.

Unencumbered by my homelessness and its literal baggage, I spent a glorious afternoon handing out newspapers at King's Cross Train Station. I felt productive again; happy again, human again. And I looked forward to completing the remaining assignments, confident my initiative and proven readiness to seek employment would fall on more understanding ears in the following week. And the money was more than welcome.

Again, silly me.

Not only was I denied permission, I was angrily informed I shouldn't be accepting paid work without their knowledge. I was accused of being secretive and not properly engaging with them. I was required to tell them everything if I wanted their help; and I was told accepting employment was not advisable as it would affect the job-seeking benefits I had (involuntarily) signed on for and prevent me from using their services.

I argued that was not what I had been told when I first signed up and had made it very plain that finding employment was my main priority. I was subsequently told that was not true, that I had agreed finding housing should be my only concern. I received the first of dozens of accusations of being "confused" that would be thrown at me over the coming months and was again informed I needed to learn to "play the game".

It was my first taste of the random Jekyll and Hyde nature of the staff and volunteers of both The Connection and later, Passage House. I immediately filed a formal complaint with one of the managers who promised to investigate. The next day there was a clear-out. More than a quarter of the storage lockers suddenly became available. The people using them had not been in contact with the charity for months –in some cases over a year. The issue had simply been overlooked. They were presumably "too busy" to check the current whereabouts of their service users.

I won the battle, but it proved a pyrrhic victory; and I had made enemies in the process. I was finally provided a locker, but not in time to allow me to show up for the second session of newspaper distribution. I was terminated for being unreliable. My beacon of hope had been unceremoniously snuffed out.

Shortly after, the Manager of their Employment, Training and Education section presented me with an internship opportunity in the Communications Department at John Lewis Department Stores. It was an opening I was keen to pursue and I spent hours honing my CV and application form with an attention to style and detail I had not applied since my days as a business journalist. I was confident my background alone would see me granted an interview at the very least. My past duties and experience matched those required for the position line for line; and my references were glowing. My application was submitted via The Connection and I was told they would inform me the minute they had a response.

Two weeks later I found out, by accident, my case worker had turned the opportunity down on my behalf without consulting me. He did not feel it was in my best interest. When I confronted him, he admitted he didn't want me to find out because it would only upset me. When I asked why he felt it wasn't in my best interest, he didn't provide any answer; simply looked at me with a mild stone-cold smile. I was getting so used to seeing these stone-cold smiles on a regular basis I was starting to recognize the different variations.

Two employment opportunities had now been lost as a result of The Connection's interference. Another however, soon presented itself; and gave every indication the third time would prove the charm. The Orwell Foundation was sponsoring a theatrical reading of George Orwell's "Down and Out in Paris and London" to be livestreamed on the Internet. Celebrities and homeless survivors were invited to read a chapter from the book, and a selection of service users from various charities in London were asked to write a brief three-minute testimonial of their experiences to be read over the course of the event. I was one of the chosen. It wasn't paid work, but it was 'charity approved.'

Over the next four days I jotted down my tale the old-fashioned pen and paper way and copied them into electronic format on the computers at The Connection and the Westminster Library. I feared going over the allotted three minutes but magnanimously informed the director she had the freedom to make any cuts she saw fit. I was not going to allow my verbosity to get in the way of art. My verbosity had other ideas however, and I surpassed the time limit with my testimony clocking in at a whopping ten minutes.

Ego. Art. It's a fine line.

Show day arrived. A who's who of English celebrities participated in the readings. I confess I didn't recognize many, but my ingrained Canadian politeness allowed me to gaze at them with the same star-struck awe reserved for those few I did. The production was engrossing; the cast and audience one of the friendliest you could encounter; and my overlong scribblings were performed as the finale, uncensored and uncut. The cast infused my words with more strength, more power, and more drama than I could ever hope to inspire. It was a hell of a performance. To top it all off my testimony had been published online by the Huffington Post the same day it was performed, accessible for all the world to see. It would be translated into French and performed in Paris later that year.

A derelict diva was born. I began scribbling notes for future literary, theatrical, possibly cinematic endeavours; and dreaming of the Emmys, Oscars, Tonys, Baftas, and Pulitzer Prizes that would adorn my mantle. Blissfully forgetting of course I was homeless and didn't even possess the proverbial pot to piss in, let alone a mantle. Nevertheless, I left the theatre confident my luck was changing for the better.

Luck, it turned out, was waiting in the wings, twirling its handlebar moustache, and snickering at my misplaced optimism. This was but an intermission. The next act had more drama to reveal.

All the Men and Women Merely Players

I'm not that strong."
　　"This is a mistake. A hiccup. A bad dream."
　　"I'm not like them."
　　"I'm not that strong."

They were my own words. Words I had committed to paper being repeated back to me two days after they had been performed on stage. Two days after they had been published online. Though I had recorded them as part of my thoughts as a freshly anointed rough sleeper, I had never actually heard them expressed by anyone else. Until that day.

I had been regularly volunteering with The Connection shortly after I had been signed into their books. It was a good way to gain favour; a good way to earn meal tickets; and a good way to learn the ins and outs of the system. Part of my duties included signing in new clients, gathering their basic information and the main reason behind their homelessness. Sometimes they were shell-shocked; sometimes they were agitated; sometimes they were cynical, familiar with the system and impatient to get the paperwork completed quickly so they could head downstairs for a shower and a meal. But never had anyone expressed the same thoughts and feelings I had, particularly as direct quotations of the very words I had penned. And each time I was quoted, the waterworks would commence –loud, fierce, and brief; the tears drying as quickly as they had started, only to reappear when my words passed his lips again.

I was puzzled at first, then suspicious. I considered the possibility he was having a quiet laugh at my sensitivity, something I was regularly teased for –sometimes affectionately, sometimes not– by the friends I had made since entering the street life. But I had never seen him before, not even in a peripheral sense. Homelessness may be a global issue affecting tens of thousands, but the numbers surrounding each shelter are generally quite small, and they often form a temporary, occasionally tight-knit community. At the very least they learn to recognize each other on sight even if they don't engage with each other. This was the first time I had seen this gentleman and, interestingly, the last. Once his sign-in process was complete he vanished, never to be seen again, not even in Trafalgar Square or Charing Cross where the bulk of The Connection's clients spent their days drinking, begging, stealing, and fighting.

After he left, one of the staff came rushing to the table in a frenzy of exuberance. She had overheard the conversation of course. I had learned by that point the staff overhear, or learn of, every conversation, no matter how private. She over-bubblingly pointed out he had used the very same words I had written. It was proof of the power of my writing, and I could use that skill to do a lot of good for other homeless people. And wasn't it wonderful The Connection had helped me discover that talent. They could help me use my skills to help others.

Setting aside the fact my previous career in journalism had already provided me with a slight inkling I might have a flair for the English language –I was a good hack writer at the very least– the entire exchange felt "off" somehow. It was the first time I felt a 'chance encounter' on charity premises was manufactured: a little real-life theatrical presentation staged for my benefit. The first time, but not the last.

I also considered the troubling possibility I was starting to grow paranoid. My trust in the people I had turned to for help was rapidly diminishing. It isn't much of a leap from distrust to paranoia, and I worried I might be in the early stages of making that jump. Until that point any issues that had arisen with the staff were matters of, in *their* words, "misunderstandings". Whether those misunderstandings were the result of misinterpretation on my part or miscommunication on theirs was open to debate. It was a concern, but one I quickly put aside as I was still hoping my theatrical debut would lead to legitimate offers of employment that would provide the stable income I needed to return to my previous flat.

Those offers had yet to reach my ears. The Connection had asked me to sign an agreement stating all enquiries resulting from the performance or the publication pass through them. They fell just short of being insistent; but offered friendly 'nudges' to encourage my agreement. They claimed they were more skilled in dealing with the media than I and only wanted to protect me. I reminded them newsprint ran in my blood, being a third-generation journalist myself, and was more than comfortable dealing with these matters. They smiled their polite "duly noted" smiles, and argued I was too vulnerable to make these decisions myself and again, their only concern was to protect me. It was ridiculous; however I had no choice but to agree as my mobile phone had been stolen from the centre just a few days previously. I had no other way to be contacted. Beggars can't be choosers. They can only sit back and let others choose for them. I signed the relevant paperwork and they promised to let me know of any job offers that came to their attention.

Much to the dismay of my Ego, only one opportunity came knocking. My pedestal of literary and theatrical glory came crashing down like the house of cards it truly was. It appeared no one outside the world of homelessness itself was interested.

Chastening myself for again allowing my dreams to supersede my station in life; I was grateful at least one person had expressed curiosity. Months later I discovered more interest had been shown than the staff at The

Connection had revealed, and more people had tried to connect with me. Those options were never brought to my attention, even when I asked. Whether that was in my best interest –or The Connection's– is open to interpretation.

The day of the interview arrived, and I met with a representative of Rogers, Coleridge & White, a literary agency based in London. It came up early in the conversation he was good friends with employees at The Connection; and was heavily involved with the No Second Night Out initiative that had left a sour taste in my mouth when I first landed in the streets. When I mentioned the flaw in their name based on my experience of eight attempts, he informed me it was a common misinterpretation. "No Second Night Out" is meant as a goal to strive for; not a promise. I was still hopeful a job was within my grasp, so shared in the chuckle over my silly "common misinterpretation" through gritted teeth.

After praising my abilities as a writer, he offered to act as my agent. He saw my role as a champion for homeless charities, naturally starting with The Connection and No Second Night Out. He would assign stories he would later submit to the newspapers he saw fit or allow the charities to use the articles themselves if the media expressed no interest. When I asked if I had the freedom to criticise the charities –I was starting to develop a few– he gushingly agreed, but under the caveat he would have complete editorial control over the final copy, and re-write any problematic areas as he saw fit.

I also told him I knew from my own experience as a Magazine Editor I didn't need an agent to make newspaper submissions; that as a general rule of thumb those were the first submissions I rejected unread. He responded with the same polite, stone faced smile I was getting used to seeing on a regular basis at The Connection. Duly noted.

We then discussed "A Knight in the Slums," and I presented the general outline: a biography of Sir John Kirk's life and an analysis of social conditions at the time. He suggested I drop the biography aspect, focus on the social conditions of Victorian London, and compare them to conditions today to promote the good work the charities do, and show the progress that had been made –by the charities of course. Personally, I was starting to question just how much progress had been made but kept that thought to myself. I again requested the freedom to criticize the charities' work, and he suddenly announced we would co-write the book together –so he could keep me on track and ensure it was written responsibly.

That was a step too intrusive. I wasn't about to let a man who was eroding my trust so quickly have editorial control over my family's life. When I asked about the pay scale, he didn't provide specific figures; simply stated it was too complicated to go into at the moment and not to worry. Another standard response I was getting used to at the Connection. He then reminded me with his winningest smile that all payments would be subject to his agency fees and co-writing credits.

I wanted to laugh in his face, but I was heartbroken. Meetings with agents do not come easily. Though I knew from experience the conditions he was proposing would have resulted in professional suicide, I was frantically trying to find some way to accept. I requested time to think about it, but ultimately turned him down. I was devastated. Another avenue of hope had been unceremoniously closed.

The staff of The Connection were not pleased.

My halcyon days of "Nudges" were over.

Rites of Initiation

There are many rites of passage to stagger through as you join the Tribe of the Homeless. Those milestones you tick off as you burrow further into the ranks of Humanity's Rejects. Finding yourself unceremoniously dumped on the streets indefinitely is obviously the first. It's frightening; but it's only the first. Anyone can do that. It is but the first step in the journey, and surprisingly banal in hindsight. It is the initiations of indignity that follow that separates the wheat from the chaff; the men from the boys; the hardened veterans from the wannabe pretenders.

There is the first time you see the look of disgust in someone's face when they unexpectedly catch you bathing in a public lavatory. That look stays burned in your memory forever. They are the eyes you recall every time you spy that look in the future. There is the humiliation you feel the first time you eliminate your bowels in a public greenery and sobbingly try to cover your crime with the surrounding dirt, realizing belatedly you have no way to wash your hands until morning. That humiliation remains embedded in the pit of your stomach for all time.

There is the first time you wake to a rainstorm in the middle of the night. Your person, your sleeping bag, and your remaining possessions drenched to capacity. They take days to dry and acquire a musty fragrance that follows you everywhere. There is the first time you awake in the night to find yourself being kicked, beaten, or robbed; either by drunken louts out for a night on the town, or by your fellow natives in the Tribe of the Homeless. There is the first time you are woken by a police patrol and forced to move your vagrancy elsewhere or risk arrest. And there is the first time you show willing to take them up on their offer, realizing it is the path to a warm bed for at least one night; and the subsequent backpedalling that proves their threat was nothing more than a posturizing feint.

The first time you steal. The first time you beg. The first time you're spat on. The first time you're kicked. The first time you are offered money to peddle drugs. The first time you're searched for them. The first time you are offered money for a sexual act. The first time you accept. The first time you find yourself unexpectedly groped by one of your friends in the Tribe, drunk to the point of delirium and motivated not by sexual desire, but a desperate need for any kind of human contact, any form of affection, any kind of misdirected balm for the loneliness. And the first time you experience the horror of watching another man's psyche shatter before you in a wailing torrent of shame, humiliation, and self-loathing when his pitiable advances are rejected. There is a first time for everything.

These are the rites that humiliate you; harden you; hack away at your soul and strip you of your humanity. And they don't end after you have been removed from the streets and placed in 'charity approved' housing. For housing is not a home. It is not the solution the public is misled into believing. It is a holding pen for Humanity's Rejects, often more dangerous than the streets themselves. Homelessness deceivingly repackaged as a successful resolution.

I have yet to achieve all these milestones, but I have ticked off many. And I have come uncomfortably close to reaching others, particularly the less salubrious rituals that see you consciously chip away at your own dignity and self-respect in order to survive. Indignities randomly inflicted on you are a dime a dozen when you're homeless. It is those indignities you *allow* yourself to suffer that really prove your mettle.

I found myself unexpectedly passing one of the smaller rites of initiation while staying in the Night Shelter at The Connection –a minor infraction compared to most other abuses and humiliations– but one that proved a major turning point in my ongoing descent.

It was shortly after 2:30 in the morning and sleep was stubbornly elusive. The caterwaul of snores had been unusually subdued, but I had not engaged in enough physical activity during the day for my body to need sleep. My mind was racing, and my limbs were restless. I tossed. I checked the time. I turned. I checked the time. I stared at the ceiling. I checked the time. I stared at the wall. I checked the time. I paced to the lavatory with no real need to use it. I checked the time. I paced back to my cot. I checked the time. It was not even 3 o'clock and morning was still an infinite three hours away.

Though I had been making valiant efforts to cut down on my smoking in the Quixotic quest to quit, I found the sheer burden of Time ... Standing ... Still to be the biggest barrier to those attempts. As the clock slumbered past 3:00 I found myself stepping outside to the basement level walkway for a cigarette, my sixth since going to bed. I had learned to make the act of rolling a cigarette a drawn-out ritual to help tick off the minutes and hoped to put that emerging skill to good use. It wasn't so much the act of smoking itself that made the addiction so difficult to beat; it was the activity that surrounded it: the ultimate make-work project of the itinerant. The art of time wasting takes more discipline than people appreciate.

I opened my tattered pouch of tobacco: a symbiotic blend of the fresh product I had purchased days previously, and the stale, sometimes crusty remains scooped from the cigarette butts I had picked up off the streets and outdoor ashtrays since then. I removed a pinch between my fingers and slowly distributed it on the rolling paper, painstakingly spreading it across the fold. I picked out the stubborn gravelly nuggets that had been mined from the discards of others, dropped them on the ground beside me, and spread the tobacco again trying to distribute it as evenly as possible. I added a filter, then picked the delicate contraption up between my thumbs and middle fingers and engaged in the act of rolling with the slow, tender deliberation of a lover. I slipped my tongue across the sealing paste leaving just enough moisture to fasten the tube without soaking the paper and making the entire endeavour useless. I pinched out the tuft of tobacco that poked through the open end and returned that precious smidgeon to my pouch.

Tapping the completed cigarette three times on its filtered end, I leaned back against the perimeter wall, placing the freshly rolled death-stick between my lips. rummaged through my trouser pocket until I found my lighter, fiddled with it between my fingers, and brought it close to my face. With a flick of my thumb I gave birth to a baby flame, applied it to the end of my tubular appendage, and waited for that familiar orange glow to indicate ignition was successful. I returned the lighter to my pocket, pinched my lips together and inhaled that melodramatic first deep plume of smoke tobacco addicts know so well. I exhaled, coughed, and took my second puff.

A drop of water suddenly splashed onto the middle of the cigarette, rendering it useless. I cursed in annoyance. Another splash struck my arm. Then another on top of my head, followed by a brief trickle that suddenly stopped. I scanned the ground for sudden spots of dew to indicate a passing rain shower and saw none. A burst pipe perhaps? I stepped away from the wall, turned around, and looked up.

To be met with a powerful stream of urine splashing on my face. And in my mouth. I jumped back, bent over and retched. To my disappointment no cleansing vomit was forthcoming and I was forced to gag on the taste of stale tobacco and fresh piss. I looked up and recognized one of the other service users as he shook the remaining droplets to the ground, laughing hysterically. He tucked himself back in his pants and skipped away from the railing, still laughing.

He was a regular client of The Connection and had been denied entry to the shelter that night for drunkenness. Clients are regularly turned away and left to their own devices whatever the season, often causing chaos in the surrounding area. However, it isn't always a straightforward refusal. Should that client die during the night from the elements or misadventure –as has happened– a charity could be subject to legal action. Often, potentially troublesome clients are officially signed in, then 'nudged' into making the decision to leave themselves. The responsibility becomes the client's; not the charity's, and the charity is freed of any legal consequences. It also helps them keep their numbers high, and their potential workloads low. Often when charities appear to be at full capacity on paper, there are many empty beds still available, claimed by those who had nudgingly decided to leave after signing in.

I ran back into the shelter screaming at the top of my lungs, waking many who had been sleeping. They weren't particularly perturbed due to the sheer entertainment value, something I had appreciated myself in the past. One of the staff did make a genuine attempt to catch the man, but by the time I had finished showering he had returned unsuccessful. The staff were genuinely sympathetic and in all fairness there was not much they could do but file a report for the Day Centre to investigate the next day.

There wasn't much of an investigation. I was told there was nothing The Connection could do about the incident as they could not be held responsible for the actions of clients outside their premises. I was also informed it was a common occurrence, and I should have known better than to stand against the perimeter wall. They advised me not to do so in the future. I filed a written suggestion they install a splash guard over part of the area to not only protect their clients from unwanted urination, but from the rain and snow. I was thanked with the ubiquitous stone-cold smile, and politely informed it was a wonderful idea they would take into consideration. Two years later a splash guard still had not been installed. I can only assume funds are better spent on an Impact and Evidence Coordinator to study the intricacies of Nudge Theory than keeping their clients dry. What do I know about charity finances? I'm only homeless.

It would be churlish to include the whispered conversation I overheard between two of the night centre staff later that same night. One had just come back from his break and informed the other his beer was hidden behind the fridge in the usual spot. Call me churlish. By this point in my relationship with The Connection nothing was surprising me anymore. I simply added the exchange to the notes I was taking with increasing regularity, not for future posterity but for future protection.

The Connection may have responded to my urinary misadventure with bored disdain but in the surrounding homeless community it was the social equivalent of my unveiling at a Debutante's Ball. No longer a wannabe pretender waiting in the wings, I had officially arrived on the scene. My piss-soaked noggin glistening like a gold-plated tiara; my ragged piss-streaked clothes billowing around me like a taffeta dress. It served as a mark of respect among those who had suffered the same indignity. Everybody wanted to be my best friend. And a best friend was exactly what I needed.

It is common for people to pair up in the streets, often people with little in common. You need someone to watch your back; someone to confide in, someone to add their skill set to yours so that together you have a fighting chance at survival. And when you're a 120-pound middle class twit who couldn't fight his way out of a damp paper bag in a rainstorm, you need a fighter with muscle. I had brains; I didn't have brawn. Without brawn, my brains weren't enough. I needed a figurative 'Partner in Crime'. For the streets are vicious, and the homeless are not as cuddly as the charities would like you to believe in their heartfelt Christmas appeals.

I was spoilt for potential suitors. The Connection had failed to enforce any justice for my urinary assault; but a couple of newly befriended street enforcers did. A few days after the incident the miscreant appeared sporting the painfully colourful bruising of a fresh black eye, cuts and bruises on his face and arms, and a limp in his right leg. His formerly cocky spark had been replaced with a sullen, downcast stare. Justice had been obtained. Street justice. I quietly approved. I quietly cheered.

Many took me under their wings, providing a rudimentary education in street smarts. I was trained in the basics of street fighting: the forehead to the nose, the knee to the groin; the punch to the kidneys; the broken bottle neck hidden in your jacket pocket "just in case." (Go for the throat.) I was given a tour highlighting the locations of every hidden CCTV camera in the surrounding area, and the even more important blind spots that are not remotely recorded. I was taught to develop my peripheral vision to better find dropped coins, wallets, cigarette butts, and other luxuries.

Though theft was a rite of passage I steadfastly refused to embrace, my conscience was more than willing to accept the ill-gotten gains of others. I ate well for the first time in weeks. My tatty socks and underpants were soon replaced with clean new undergarments deftly lifted from the finest stores Oxford Street had to offer. It wasn't long before my coquettish acceptance of these stolen tokens of friendship turned proactive. A casually dropped need or request dropped into a group conversation almost guaranteed delivery before the end of the day. I began to offer my computer skills in exchange for whatever plunder I required at any given time: a valuable service in the chaotic bartering economy of the homeless. I was learning just how easy life in the streets could be if you allowed your morality to slip even a little; especially if the morality of others is there for the taking.

Hypocrisy, thy name is Peter. And I still have the Union Jack mug to prove it.

My eating habits had improved. My fashion sense had improved. But I still needed a 'Partner in Crime'. I still needed muscle. Skilled muscle. Brawn is nothing more than window-dressing if the owner doesn't know how to use it. That narrowed my choices down exponentially. And we had to get along; be able to converse, joke around, banter; feel comfortable in each other's company. In short, we actually had to be friends. That whittled my options even more. At the time, and even in hindsight, it was the easiest of decisions.

I made my choice.

Poorly, as it turned out.

"Where Dreams Go To Die"

After declining the only employment offer allowed to reach my ears, I started receiving regular advice to stop looking for work as The Connection staff were suddenly concerned for my mental health. Staff, volunteers, and even clients would suddenly stop me and ask if I was feeling alright with looks of great concern. I was told I had to admit I had a problem before anybody could help me. What that problem was exactly was never made clear, but nobody could help me until I admitted it. A confusingly mind-twisting little Catch 22 to ponder as I wiled away the snore-filled nights.

The pressure to apply for housing benefits also increased. I again reminded my case worker I had no need for housing assistance as a friend had lent me money to cover my rent at my former residence once The Connection helped me find employment. He informed me my situation had changed. I should not be looking for work and my 28-day limit for staying in the night shelter had long expired. They were bending the rules by allowing me to stay, and for that I should be thankful. I asked if they would really put me back on the streets and was told

"That's not what I'm saying, I'm just saying you won't be allowed to stay here." When I pointed out the Orwellian double-speak, I was told I was being silly, and reminded once again how grateful I should be for the help they had already provided. I needed to show willing or I wouldn't be allowed to use their facilities.

Unnerved, I agreed to look at a studio flat in Orpington. I asked why it was so far away and was informed I did not fit the criteria to be housed in London. I asked what that criteria consisted of and was told it was too complicated to get into. He was too busy. When I restated I could easily return to my former flat once I could confirm regular payment of rent, I was told the system does not operate like that. Repeated attempts to ascertain how the system operated remained unanswered beyond the now common refrains of: "Don't worry about it;" "It's too complicated;" "We know what we're doing," or the increasingly chilling stone-faced smile.

Two days later I arrived at the house and wryly noticed I didn't need the specific number to find it. The yard and exterior of the building were in such a state of disrepair compared to the other buildings on the street it was comically obvious. The uneven dirt and gravel were colourfully punctuated with a few patches of brown grass that had grown past my waist. The dozens of beer cans overflowing from the rubbish bins and scattered around the front yard proved a nice decorative touch, as was the broken bowl of mouldy cat-food on the front step. The smell of stale kitty litter dominated the entryway. Closer examination revealed a pile consisting of three latex gloves, two hypodermic needles and a rubber tube. Presumably kitty had a drug habit. A mouldy dog bed and battered rental bike were propped against the side wall. I would find these were all surprisingly common features of 'charity approved' housing –only the colour of the front door's chipped paint and brands of beer changed.

There were three other people waiting, all sent from different homeless charities. We had shown up well before the appointed time. One man was drunk. The second, covered in scars and rashes, was graphically describing the various illnesses from which he suffered, pausing only to urinate on the front of the house. The third, surveying the dereliction we were standing in, took a drag off his joint and quipped, "This is a place where dreams go to die."

It was a great line. I quickly slipped away to discretely jot it down for future literary posterity and noticed the following sign attached to all the lampposts on both sides of the street:

"£10,000 reward for information leading to the arrest and conviction of persons responsible for the killing and mutilation of cats, rabbits and foxes in Greater London, Surrey, Hampshire, Kent, Berkshire, Sussex, Manchester, West Midlands, Oxfordshire, Hertfordshire, Northamptonshire and Buckinghamshire.

"If you find any mutilated bodies or body parts please contact SNARL at ……"

Clearly one of England's finer neighbourhoods.

A half hour after the appointed meeting time, the letting agent phoned to say he would be late. He couldn't find the house. When he finally arrived almost an hour after the phone call, my pot-smoking companion with the Shakespearean wit recognized him, but not fondly.

"No way! No fucking way," he yelled. "I'm not getting screwed by you fuckers again!" He stormed away, shoving the agent and kicking a car as he raged down the street leaving a tempest of the most delightfully foul curses in his wake.

It wasn't a good omen.

The flat itself proved to be as "distinct" as the yard. It was filthy. Rubbish from the previous tenant was still scattered on the floor and countertop. No effort had been made to sweep the floor or wipe down the walls. The agent was apologetic and assured us he would look into the matter. That claim would prove to be as common in future viewings as beer cans in the front yard. There was rarely any attempt made to even pick rubbish off the floor before a viewing. In some cases the smell of mould was stomach-churning, but after the standard apology and promise to look into the matter, you were offered the assurance it would be easy to clean after you settled in, and the guarantee of stores within walking distance to purchase the necessary supplies.

With the viewing complete, it was time for the negotiations to commence. This consisted of the agent stating if anyone was interested in accepting the flat, the contract would have to be signed immediately as there were other viewings and it would be claimed by the end of the day. When I asked to look at the lease agreement, I was informed there was no need for me to see it as the charity would take care of it. I insisted on seeing it and was answered with a curt "No." I asked a third time and was ignored completely. I wasn't even granted the courtesy of a stone-faced smile. Amazingly, one of the remaining viewers –the sick one- agreed to take it. "I've seen worse," he shrugged. To be fair, experience would prove him right. I would see worse over the coming months.

After the viewing, I ran into the gentleman who had stormed off as we both waited for the train back to London. After declining the joint he offered I asked him about his previous experience with the letting agency. He said he had been housed with them a couple of years previously after splitting up with his girlfriend and was still paying off the debt he incurred. There had been a security deposit and administration fees he had not been told about. He had also been told by his charity the landlord would be responsible for paying the council tax, then found out months later he was responsible and was in debt to the local council. The leasing agency had regularly added service charges and penalty fees without warning, cutting into the already meagre amount of benefits he was being paid. They then evicted him for falling behind on those payments. He was still in debt to both the council and the agency; and had to regularly attend court as they attempted to receive their restitution from his benefit money.

I wasn't sure what to make of his account. It sounded slightly ludicrous, but the details were specific enough to have an air of truth about them. He probably wasn't revealing all the facts relating to his situation, particularly those relating to his role or his own actions. And his marijuana use was more than likely a key factor in his financial woes. But I had to remind myself not to let my middle-class snobbery relating to his drug use invalidate his claims. And his intention was sincere: he didn't want others to get caught in the same trap. He had nothing to gain by advising a stranger he would never see again.

I returned to London and related the conversation to one of the staff members who had sat me down for a spontaneous chat –not a formal meeting, just a friendly "chat." She told me there was no truth to it and not to listen to what my homeless friends at The Connection said. When I clarified it wasn't a friend but a stranger who was genuinely concerned about the future welfare of another person, our friendly chat came to an abrupt close with a smile. The stone cold one.

A few days later she sat me down for another informal "chat" to thank me for sharing my concerns about the leasing agency with her. The staff had held a meeting and it had transpired they had heard similar stories. She informed me they were no longer dealing with that agency and to put aside any worries I might have about potentially renting from them. She couldn't share any details with me just yet, but The Connection had something else in mind to help me.

That statement alone filled me with an ominous sense of dread. And the entire exchange proved to be yet another 'performance' staged for my benefit, peppered with lies. A month later a friend was sent to a viewing on property owned by the same landlords. Over a year later The

Connection were still sending clients to properties owned by that agency. They hadn't ended the business relationship at all. They had lied. Again.

That first dip into the murky waters of 'charity approved' housing proved an eye-opener and added to my increasing concerns surrounding the 'processing' of the homeless community.

Meat is processed. The homeless deserve better.

And if they don't shuffle willingly to their slaughter. . .

A Pawn for the Playing

I didn't see it coming.

Despite my growing unease I was still offering my services as a volunteer. I had lost faith in The Connection but wanted to stay in their good books as the relationship deteriorated. I was scared. Scared of angering them further. Scared of being returned to the streets. Scared the remaining time I had to find a job and return home to Canada was fading quickly. Volunteering and participating in their programmes were the best way to "show willing"; even if just to buy myself enough time to figure out a solution to my predicament. Besides the free meal tickets were helpful; an enticing carrot to ensure my voluntary subservience no matter the circumstances. I did not want to lose them.

I was still helping with their morning sign-in procedures when their Client Involvement Co-ordinator (Another lovely job title with another lovely salary. It too looks good on the curriculum vitae.) sat down for a "casual chat" to see how I was doing. She had been one of the driving forces behind my "Down and Out Live" participation as well as the friend of the literary agent that had presented me with my lone, non-paying job proposition.

With a cheerful, non-confrontational disposition, she often came down from the upstairs offices to engage in friendly 'chats' with the clients. She was everybody's 'friend'. Lava wouldn't melt in her mouth, let alone butter; and I was still stupid enough to trust her.

She asked how I felt after turning down the opportunity they had arranged as she was concerned I wasn't taking it well. I admitted to being disappointed; and hurt that it had been the only prospect that had surfaced. She admitted to disappointment as well –disappointed for me of course, she pointedly added– but reminded me I should be excited they had helped me discover my skill for writing. These continual reminders to credit them for discovering a talent I already knew I possessed were grating. They may as well have demanded praise for telling me I was five foot six, had blue eyes, and spoke with a Canadian accent. They weren't exactly leading me into exciting new territories of self-discovery. Still, it was her salary to earn.

The chat then turned to the writing process itself. She found it fascinating and wanted to get inside the brain of a writer. I happily –stupidly– complied. I explained how I took a Jungian approach to my work; that I was nothing more than an over glorified pen, leaving myself open to the collective human unconscious that sometimes gives resonance to a piece if it is fortunate enough to connect to those basic human experiences and emotions that unite us all. It is a process of absorbing your experiences, processing them, letting them sink into your subconscious mind and marinate before even thinking about committing them to paper.

I could have shut up. I should have shut up. But it is a topic I enjoy discussing and I didn't shut up. The words kept flowing from my lips, providing bullets for the metaphorical gun my mouth was now aiming at my foot and preparing to fire.

I described how it was comparable to an addiction; how on those rare occasions when the words flow without effort, the mental, emotional and physical rush delivers a euphoria that can't be properly explained to those who have not been blessed with the experience. That nine times out of ten the words don't flow; and the frustration and anger and crumpled up sheets of paper thrown at the wall generally inspire a vow to never write again. But it's those rare times they do flow that keep you coming back to the words; keep you scribbling; keep you suffering the agonies of writing in the hope you will again re-capture that elusive state of ecstasy. It's the ultimate high.

BANG!

I admitted that I had had so much to process since landing on the streets it was a bit overwhelming: an information overload. That the sheer volume of experiences in such a short period of time, good and bad, were almost too much to get my head around. That the intensity of the emotions –the fear, the pain, the uncertainty, the not knowing who to trust or believe– was crushing at times. Caught up in the informality of the chat and my own narcissistic pleasure in discussing the applications of Jungian Theory to my faux-humble calling as a hack chronicler of the human experience, I jokingly confessed: "It's driving me nuts."

BANG!

Her eyes, that had glazed over during my loquacious meanderings –as most eyes do when I loquaciously meander– suddenly lit up. Her excitement was glowing, her smile as blinding as headlights. "So you admit to having mental health issues," she gushed. "That's great!"

I made a valiant, ultimately unsuccessful effort to backpedal, but I had been caught so off-guard by her reaction, and unsure of the reason behind it, that I stammered self-defensive gibberish like a child caught with his hand in a cookie jar. "I was talking about myself as a writer; not as a person," I tried to clarify. "They're like two different people." (*BANG!*) I tried to explain that even though I felt overwhelmed at times, I had never been embarrassed to stay in touch with my emotions and wasn't afraid to take myself alone somewhere for a good cry. (*BANG!*) I was so rattled, the surge of adrenaline brought on the physical trembling that had already been mis-identified as a sign of possible addiction inherited from my mother.

Her eyes, alert after their shift from boredom to excitement, shifted again to overdramatic sympathy. "There's nothing to be ashamed of," she cooed soothingly, as if talking to a simpleton. "A lot of writers have mental health issues. It's great you've finally admitted it." Her eyes shifted again to perky delight before suddenly remembering a meeting she had to attend. She picked up her notebooks and digital tablet and left, leaving me sitting there, jaw dropped to the floor, trying to figure out exactly what the hell had just happened.

A couple of days later my case worker sat me down to inform me the staff had held a meeting and come up with a solution to my "problem". Recognizing yet another disturbing pattern I asked why I wasn't present at these meetings as I obviously had a vested interest: it was *my* future being discussed. As was proving the case with awkward questions, it was waved away without a proper answer. "Too busy." "Too complicated." "You wouldn't understand." "We have your best interest at heart." All interchangeable; all meaningless, but all imparting the same message: Ask me no questions; I'll tell you no lies.

He had more subtle lies to weave.

At this meeting, the staff had decided to arrange an interview for me with an organization called Assisted Accommodation at their office in Wood Green. They had taken my concerns about my first viewing to heart, and my case worker assured me this new residence would be nothing like the previous. It was staffed 24 hours, maintained high standards of cleanliness, and security was present to allay my safety concerns –concerns The Connection knew were a high priority for me. I would be safe, I would be looked after, and I would get all the support I needed. There was, however, a catch, two in fact. I had to admit I was not looking for work. And I had to allow them to help with my mental health issues.

He was so soothing the sun wouldn't have melted in his mouth, let alone lava. And though he had strategically sugar-coated the specifics I had a reasonably clear idea exactly what type of accommodation the staff had decided to place me in and refused immediately. I reiterated finding work was my number one priority. I needed it not only to get back on my feet, but to begin making payments on my debt in Canada before I returned; and to continue those payments while I sought employment there. I was under the mistaken belief that because of my British Citizenship I would be arrested on my return. It would be more than two years before I found out this would not have been the case. To this day I still kick myself for failing to apply one of the fundamental tenets of journalism to my personal situation: always double check your facts with an independent source.

Hindsight aside, his reply genuinely shocked me. He told me to stop worrying about the debt. It was only adding to my issues. I didn't have to pay it. He said the solution was to wait seven or ten years and the debt would automatically be cleared. I could then return with a clean slate. I was appalled at the suggestion in itself; but picked up on the one flaw in his strategy. I was not a Canadian Citizen, merely a Permanent Resident. I had, at that point, only nine months remaining before I lost the right to return. He told me I was being difficult just for the sake of being difficult.

As is often the case with charity staff, he talked *at* me; not allowing a single opportunity for reaction. Not communicating so much as chanting words –the same words repeated ad nauseum –over and over and over again. A wall of words, as effective as the proverbial wall of brick. Unyielding. Unbending, Immovable. Through all my charity experiences I repeatedly found myself beating my head against a brick wall of words.

He told me my main problem is I am "too independent". It was admirable, but I needed to accept I could no longer look after myself. I shouldn't be working. I was sick. I needed help. I needed rest. It wasn't my fault. I had nothing to be ashamed of. I had already admitted I had problems just a few days ago and it was time to take the next step. It was time to put myself in the hands of professionals. They would look after me. There was nothing to be afraid of. I had nothing to be ashamed of. Word after word after word; brick after brick after brick.

The unfortunate truth is I *was* questioning my mental health and had been since my own words were quoted to me after the "Down and Out" performance. At that time, I wondered if I was starting to veer into paranoia and reading into the situation a little too much. Those suspicions had taken root in the back of my mind and were slowly spreading. I *was* tense. I *was* tired. My tremors were occurring with greater regularity and I was starting to experience mild anxiety attacks. I was growing increasingly flustered and short-tempered. I attributed it to the stress of homelessness and increasing tensions with The Connection but was starting to consider the possibility that maybe there was more to it than that. Maybe they were right. Maybe there were underlying mental issues that were starting to assert themselves. My situation should have been a quick fix: find work and get back on my feet. The staff at The Connection had stated that themselves when I first signed in –with the oft-repeated caveat there are "no guarantees". But over two months later that fix was further out of my reach than it had been at the start. Maybe the tensions with staff *were* the result of misinterpretations on my part. Maybe I *was* more confused than I thought. Maybe it was me.

But I still didn't think these potential issues were severe enough to warrant the kind of arrangement I suspected was being proposed. I still believed I was functional. And I still believed finding work was the solution and I would be fine once I was back on my feet again. I was filled with growing doubt, but I remained firm and rejected his proposed solution again.

His smile remained, but his tone shifted considerably. "I don't think you understand," he said. "I'm not telling you, you don't have a choice; but you don't have *much* of a choice." If I didn't give this serious consideration I could no longer stay at The Connection. I needed to admit I needed help, or they couldn't help me. They weren't forcing me to do anything; it was my choice to make. He was just telling me the choices that were available.

It was a hell of a 'Nudge,' and that was the moment my sardonic disdain for these people turned to outright fear. I was presented a choice that wasn't really a choice, backed up by a threat that wasn't really a threat. Knowingly make a fraudulent claim about my health and lie about my ability to return to work full-time; or return to the streets without being allowed access to the "help" The

Connection –or the government– provides. I had no choice but to go with the 'Nudge.'

He accompanied me on that first interview with Assisted Accommodation, to be supportive and to help with some of the more difficult questions. We arrived early, and as we stepped out of the transit station in Wood Green he announced, "Welcome to your new home," and walked me through the area pointing out all the benefits it had to offer: a library, a movie theatre, a shopping precinct, a supermarket, a book store. All the time making reference to this being my new home, my new start. I was quietly terrified, and my tremors slowly resurfaced, reminding us both of their presence.

They continued throughout the interview itself and highlighted by my case worker as proof of my mental disorders. I remained surprisingly detached throughout the whole process, resigned to the fate I suspected The Connection had arranged. I saw no way out and spent most of the consultation sullen and withdrawn, nodding or providing monosyllabic agreement to my case worker's assertions when prompted. I initially tried to catch the interviewer's attention to give him some kind of indication this was wrong, to try to indicate I wanted to speak to him alone; but quickly abandoned those efforts when I realized my subtle signals and gesturing eyes probably weren't helping my efforts to defend my mental state.

The meeting came to a conclusion and I was assured I had done very well. It was a brave step I was taking. The staff at Assisted Accommodation would review my case with the staff of The Connection, and if successful I would be invited back for a second interview. They were confident I would be back. As we left the building my case worker congratulated me and told me how proud he was. I was finally learning. We conducted another tour of Wood Green so I could see my new home again and appreciate how lovely it was. He even bought me a coffee, stressing he was paying out of his own pocket.

In all honesty I was relieved. The wait bought me time, and the pressure at The Connection abated considerably. I made the best use of that period to make alternative arrangements before the second interview came to pass. I contacted Crisis, Shelter and St. Mungo's again by email to ask their assistance. As with my first attempts when I initially found myself homeless, those emails went unanswered. I also took steps to file complaints with the Charity Commission, the Mayor of London's office, and Citizens Advice Bureaus. Again, no response. The waiting time quickly ended and the day of the second interview came to pass. I was provided with a one-way public transit ticket and sent on my way like a child being sent to his first day of school. To my delight, I was unaccompanied.

I arrived with guns blazing. Loud, angry, and foul-mouthed, I came closer to firing a fatal shot into my foot than I was aware. For as I soon discovered, there is no second interview. It was moving-in day. The second interview is simply a small, and understandable, ruse to guide clients into their new living arrangements, where the staff were prepared should those clients prove unco-operative. This was more than the pastoral shelter my case worker had painted. This was strict accommodation for people with serious addiction or mental health issues; who require 24-hour monitoring; who are often incapable of cooking or cleaning up after themselves without supervision; who need strict rules and regulations. My histrionic curse-laden grand entrance did nothing to disprove my candidacy for such accommodation. I was gently steered into a small room and provided a seat. I was offered a glass of water which I gladly accepted. It wasn't until the door closed behind me and I heard the click of the lock that I thought, "Uh-oh."

But something I said in my rambling tirade must have struck the right note. After a few minutes a representative of Assisted Accommodation brought me a glass of water and sat at the table across from me; no notebook, no tablet, no paperwork. He asked if I was feeling better, and when I replied in the affirmative asked me to start at the beginning and tell him everything. To take all the time I needed and not to worry if I grew upset in the telling. He would be upset too in my position. I scanned his face for the ubiquitous stone-cold smile, but it wasn't there. He looked genuinely attentive. So I started at the beginning, and over the next half-hour told him everything.

He was appalled, but not surprised; angry, but sympathetic. With frank honesty he admitted homeless charities often abuse their services in this way. It is a serious issue that prevents people who genuinely need their support from getting it, and often encourages people to make fraudulent claims to receive the money from mental health benefits that living in their accommodation requires. It was plainly obvious to him I did not qualify, and I was more than capable of taking employment. He promised to file a complaint against The Connection, and though he couldn't do much to help in my current situation, told me to hang in there. He asked me to let him know when I was back on my feet.

I have yet to contact him.

I dodged a bullet that day. More than one if you factor my gun-toting mouth into the equation. Unfortunately, though it had temporarily run out of ammunition, my mouth wasn't finished quite yet. It rarely is.

Our Bread and Butter

I returned to The Connection and the atmosphere remained tense. The stone-cold smiles had gone the way of the friendly nudges, and the comments surrounding my mental health intensified. I was forced to sign into the night shelter on a daily basis, never knowing if I would be allowed entry. My days there were numbered –well into the single digit range.

Without telling a soul I quietly took myself to the Crisis office on Commercial Street, not only for assistance but to enlighten them about The Connection in the hopes they could take action against them. I explained my situation and we devised a plan to accommodate me in one of their associated night shelters and sign up for their job search programmes. I left feeling cautiously optimistic I was finally on the right path to pulling myself out of this nightmare.

Only to have the rug pulled out from under me yet again.

The next day I sat down in the common area for an impromptu chat with one of The Connection's other case workers. She was a person with whom I had a frosty relationship, and pointedly kept my distance. Weeks previously I had tried to give her a simple message from a client who was unable to attend a meeting she had scheduled for that day. Her response was so rude and aggressive I filed a written complaint, and she had to formally apologize as a result. I was not her favourite person.

She slid a two-page document on the table and told me to sign. I picked it up to read and she whisked it out of my hands telling me to just sign it. I asked what it was, and she explained it was a document stating we were having this conversation. I pointed to an area that hadn't been filled in and she said it wasn't important, she would fill it in later. I refused until I knew exactly what I was agreeing to and her face suddenly turned fierce. "Quit playing games and just sign it!" she snarled. I was momentarily terrified and signed.

She then informed me she heard I had been to Crisis. That took me aback as I had not told anyone about my meeting with them, not even my 'Partner in Crime.' She told me in no uncertain terms I should not have done that; I was sneaky and deceitful; and was trying to play one charity off the other. It was disgusting because all they had tried to do was help me and I had fought them every step of the way.

She then announced I was being moved to Passage House. I had wasted two housing opportunities and had to accept this one or I would be declaring myself voluntarily homeless. I knew Passage House by reputation. It provides temporary accommodation for the homeless, predominantly those with serious addiction issues. Its standing even within the battle-hardened homeless community was fear-provoking.

I sputtered I couldn't go there. I wasn't an addict. I had made arrangements with Crisis and just needed a couple more days to transfer to them. She announced Crisis wouldn't help me, and said, "Anyway, you've already agreed," and patted the form between us. My response was indecorous to say the least.

"You fucking *BITCH!*" I screamed loud enough to throw the entire room into silence.

BANG!

That wasn't just the echo of my mouth scoring another direct hit on my foot; it was the sound of my hands slamming the table as I stood up and stormed out of the suddenly hushed room. Once outside, I asked a friend to roll a cigarette because my hands were shaking too hard. I started employing deep breathing techniques to settle my nerves: in through the nose, out through the mouth; in through the nose; out through the mouth. The purity of the London air was soon joined by the even more calming effects of tobacco as I accepted the hastily rolled cigarette.

I was finally starting to calm down when another staff member came out for a cigarette herself. Her actual job description was unknown, but she was another Charity Jekyll, everybody's friend, always willing to lend a sympathetic ear.

She had seen my outburst and come to learn why I was so upset. Angrily, but calmly at first, I explained what had happened. I told her I was fed up with their housing obsession, and it was obvious they couldn't help me. My main concern had always been employment and not finding a roof over my head. I had finally taken steps with a charity I believed could help, and they had just prevented me from dealing with them. Growing louder, I asked why they kept trying to force me into housing I didn't need. She quickly blurted, "Because it's our bread and butter! Why don't you get that?"

"You should have told me that from the start!" I screamed. "And sent me somewhere else! You fucking cunts! You're all fucking cunts!"

BANG!

I didn't grow physically violent, but it was another bullet hole in my increasingly perforated foot. For I had learned early on to never let your emotions show, not let anyone get under your skin. Never let them see you get angry, and never let them see you cry. They will use it against you. It was one of the first lessons of the street imparted not only by my 'Partner in Crime' but by other friends I had made. A lesson drilled into me even before the smashing of a wine bottle and my presentation with its broken neck to keep in my jacket pocket –just in case. An event in no way as ceremonial as it sounds. Just quick and practical. The homeless aren't trying to launch the Titanic; they're trying to keep themselves from drowning. (Go for the throat.)

And I had seen the truth of the lesson many times, not only between staff and clients, but between the police and rough sleepers in the semi-regular altercations and exchanges that occurred between them. Pleasant exchanges are as pleasant as any. But introduce the slightest element of conflict, or the slimmest of disagreements and the dynamics shift dramatically in favour of the authority figures. They start pressing emotional buttons, pulling psychological strings, delivering vague statements that can be construed as veiled threats, or observations that can easily be taken as insults.

It is all part of the unpromoted psychological warfare that is waged between social workers and clients behind closed charity doors, and on the streets between the vagrants and protectors of the peace walking their beats. Part of the 'processing' that is not caught on camera or recorded in the "official" accounts –only the emotional, sometimes violent reactions they provoke. Like siblings in the back seat of a car, one pokes, kicks, pull faces and taunts the other, unseen by their parents, waging a campaign of provocation for however long it takes until they get the reaction they desire.

WHACK!

The other retaliates. The bully cries victim. The car stops, punishment is administered, and the 'victim' –the true villain– is lauded as a hero. It is one of many "games" the homeless are expected to play if they want to be helped. The sport of childish backseat bullying not caught in the rear-view mirror. Submit to it with quiet stoicism –or you lose. It is merely annoying when your sibling plays the game; it is downright dangerous when that game is used as part of an organized process.

I stormed off to Trafalgar Square to calm myself again and jot these recent developments down in the hope someone would eventually listen. I phoned Crisis to inform them of the situation and was told they are not allowed to interfere with the work of other charities. I pointed out this was blatantly wrong and possibly illegal. And I asked why they had led me to believe they could help when I met with them. She reiterated they could not interfere with the work of other charities. She added the important thing is I wouldn't be sleeping on the streets and disconnected, eager to take her next call.

I gave serious consideration to doing just that, and in hindsight wish I had. After the initial shock, sleeping rough is surprisingly easy. However, in being labelled voluntarily homeless –willingly or unwillingly– you cut yourself off from all government support and assistance. I noted on a scrap of paper I kept in my back pocket at the time the correlation between benefits and drug addiction. These charity workers, who were immersed in the world of addiction and knew its ins and outs like the back of their hands, had done nothing but push me into signing up for benefits I truly didn't need at the time. Once I had become dependent on those benefits, they –and later the government– repeatedly threatened to suspend them through sanctions –essentially for not doing what I was told, whether those instructions were in my best interest or not. The charity workers were, in my mind, using the same 'get them hooked, then control them' tactics of drug dealers. And I was in the early stages of being hooked.

To this day I regret not having the courage to walk away from the system entirely and find some other way out of my predicament. Many do, and many succeed.

Their bravery deserves more praise, and more public attention, than people know. Their stories need to be heard.

I however, was not as brave, and a few days later found myself entering Passage House. I had never felt so frightened in my life.

I had yet to discover what real fear is.

Hell's Passage

They started as they meant to go on. Relentless, merciless, unyielding. No sympathy. No compassion. No respite. I *would* comply –willingly, unwillingly, broken or not –it didn't matter. I would comply. At the Connection I was merely treated like a naughty child, spoken to with the condescending manner one reserves for a simpleton, chastised with supercilious pomposity for failing to do as I was told, for failing to "play the game". I soon longed for those simpler times. At Passage House I was spoken to with open contempt and treated with scorn. No longer a naughty child, I was a figure of disgust. Welcome to Hell; unofficially sanctioned by the good Christian prelates and patrons of St. Vincent's Church.

Less than an hour after my arrival I was presented with their agreement and told to sign. I asked to read it and they asked why –it wasn't necessary. They were busy and didn't have time for this. After some discussion I pointed out it was my legal right, and after being informed I was just being difficult, I was allowed a few minutes to look it over. I circled my concerns and put question marks beside them. Under their conditions I was not allowed to accept paid work, had to agree to apply for housing benefits to pay for their temporary accommodation, and accept whatever housing they deemed to be in my best interest. I was not going to sign without those concerns being addressed.

In the discussion that followed I re-iterated, as I had dozens of times before, finding employment was my number one priority. I needed to earn an income not only to re-establish my independence, but to begin making payments on the credit card debt I had incurred in Canada during my time in England. I repeated I did not require housing assistance as I could return to my previous residence once I could guarantee payment of rent – again, all dependent on finding work. I also asked for a copy of the contract for my own records. I was told my concerns didn't matter. If I didn't sign, I would have to leave the premises immediately.

I pointed out I was being forced to sign under the threat of being returned to the streets. This argument had come up at The Connection, and I received the same double-speak in response. They were not threatening me, they were simply telling me the consequences of my actions. They were not forcing me to return to the streets, I simply wouldn't be allowed to stay there. I could look for work, but I couldn't accept it. And I shouldn't be looking for work anyway because of my mental health issues. The sooner I admitted I needed *their* help, the easier it would be for everyone. The same words; the same brick wall.

I was scared. I signed. Over the next few days, I repeatedly asked for answers to the concerns I had expressed; and requested my own copy of the contract. They responded with the usual delaying tactics of "Too busy," and "Later," before informing me my concerns didn't really matter as I had already signed. I had to abide by their rules, or I would be breaching their agreement and have to leave.

Two work opportunities came up shortly after my arrival, both the result of my testimony written for the performances of "Down and Out Live". The Editor at the Huffington Post who had commissioned the publication of my work had since taken a new position working for the London based Metro newspaper. She contacted me on a social media site and requested a meeting. It was during our discussion that I discovered far more interest had been shown in my piece, and more people had wanted to contact me than the single 'opportunity' the Connection had arranged. I had simply not had that information passed on to me from the staff, even when I specifically asked. I was disgusted. She wasn't surprised.

For she had had experiences with homelessness and their respective charities as a child and knew herself how they operated. She was empathetic to my situation and wanted me to write some pieces –weekly if possible, but she understood the daily stress that homelessness brings and didn't want to add the pressures of deadlines to that. These articles would be published on the Metro's website, and I was free, in fact encouraged, to criticize the charities as I saw fit. We discussed the terms of payment and they were more than reasonable; not enough to get me back on my feet, but a financially healthy first step on that path. I was delighted to accept.

The other opportunity had been arranged by the producer of the "Down and Out Live" production. She recommended me to the Casting Connection, one of many agencies that provide extras to cinematic productions. I had also registered for a course in Public Speaking at the City of Westminster College shortly after my theatrical debut, and though the course had yet to start, the two pursuits would perfectly entwine for further, more regular employment opportunities down the line. The pay was even better than the writing assignments and I self-effacingly chuckled at the realization that people would pay more for me to stand and say nothing than to unleash my voice on the world.

I hadn't told anyone about either of these opportunities, not my friends, not even my 'Partner in Crime'. I wanted them to be fait accompli before sharing the good news. I quietly began organizing the notes I had been taking and jotting more to lay the foundation stones for future articles. I secretly took myself to St. James Park to take the necessary self-portraits and body measurements for my casting profile. For the first time in months I was hopeful my ordeal was in the early stages of ending. Not just hopeful, excited.

Then my case worker requested a meeting.

Somehow, she had found out about the work I had accepted and told me I could not pursue it or I would have to leave. She accused me of being secretive, deceitful, and not keeping them informed of my activities. I responded, obnoxiously, that I had simply been pursuing opportunities as I had been told I could, and two happened to bear fruit. I had to accept them so I could begin earning money to start payments on my debt and return to Canada before my deadline as a Permanent Resident expired.

She told me I needed to get over my obsession with Canada. It wasn't healthy. I was in England now, and had to play by their rules.

That particular assertion did not sit well, and the argument grew heated. I shouted this was abuse, that both The Connection and Passage House are abusing the people they help, and I threatened to report them to the police, the government, and the media. I was angry, frightened, and forgot once again the cardinal rule about letting emotions show. The accompanying surge of adrenaline brought my Kirk-inherited tremors into full view and I began shaking uncontrollably.

She picked up on it right away. "You're shaking!" she screamed. "Are you on drugs? Get out! Don't come back! Just get out!"

It was one of the few requests made by any charity with which I was more than happy to comply.

I ran out of Passage House in the throes of a full-fledged panic attack. Shaking, sweating, crying, hyperventilating, heart pounding, head swimming, nauseous and close to fainting. I half-ran, half-staggered through the streets to get as far away as I could, realizing that to any and all passers-by I looked like a junkie caught in the delirium of a bad trip. I tried phoning my 'Partner' but was incomprehensible. He told me to meet him at St. James Park.

The panic attack had almost burnt itself out by the time we met, and he was able to settle my nerves to a more manageable level. I apologized for not only letting my emotions show, but for letting them explode out of control; and not just with charity staff, but with him. He said it was fine. Everyone knew I was sensitive, but the streets would toughen me up. He said it was okay to cry; he often cried himself, but to be careful about letting others see. He assured me any time I needed "to blub" I could trust him. He stayed true to his word over the coming months and was always available for support whenever the tears needed to flow. In fact, he often encouraged them.

He had been having his own difficulties with the charities and, like many homeless veterans, had decided not to make use of their shelters and sleep on the streets, choosing only to sign in to the day centres to make use of the showers and lunches while waiting for housing to be provided. As I had been thrown out and told not to return, I was frightened of being back on the streets with no recourse to help. He assured me I could camp out with him, I would be safe under his protection, and we would figure something out together. We spent the rest of the afternoon at Trafalgar Square listening to, and sometimes heckling the buskers with our other comrades in homeless arms.

I was keen to record the interaction as quickly as possible while it was still fresh in my mind but had left

Passage House empty handed. One of my other friends rose to the occasion and filched a notepad and pens from the local Ryman's Stationary Store. I accepted with a conscience as clear as ice. The notepad wasn't particularly to my liking: the cover was a shade of purple I didn't care for –("It's not purple; it's mauve ya ungrateful fuck," he responded with not entirely mock indignation.)– but I accepted the ill-gotten implements with genuine appreciation. Beggars can't be choosers, particularly when they don't have the courage to thieve for themselves.

That evening I received an apologetic phone-call from my case worker. She was sorry for upsetting me and worried I had left with the wrong impression. I was welcome to return and she asked me to come back that night to talk things over. She had stayed long after her shift had ended because she was worried. She wanted to apologize and make sure I was alright. She sounded sincere, sounded like she was on the verge of crying herself, but I snottily told her I would think about it and disconnected. After conferring with my friends, I returned.

I was taken into a room with my case worker and one of the voluntary staff. The welcoming smile vanished as the door clicked shut, replaced by an angry glare. I went to sit, and she told me to stay where I was. She declared she had not thrown me out. I had been high on drugs and left violently of my own accord after threatening her. She said she had a witness –the volunteer now standing by her side, sternly nodding. The woman had not been present for the exchange. No one had. The sterile chill of unfiltered fear spread throughout my body.

"You're lying," I murmured.

"No I'm not," she snarled. "You're the liar! Everyone knows you're a liar! And it doesn't matter...

"... Nobody's going to believe you anyway because you're homeless!"

That was the first moment to break me. No mere crack in the façade, a core part of my psyche simply broke away and shattered on the metaphysical floor beneath us. Mentally I shut down. Physically I felt an emptiness expand within me. Emotionally I felt nothing. For a few brief moments that spanned eternity I stood there, numb, until a horror unlike any I had ever known took root in the emptiness and spread throughout my entire being.

It wasn't just the audacity of the statement; it wasn't just the malice in her eyes; it was the terrifying realization that she was right. She had the power to turn fiction into reality. She had created a scenario that bore no relation to the facts as they had transpired –even produced a corresponding witness that wasn't present at the time– and everyone would believe her. She controlled the narrative. She controlled the paperwork. Her truth would be accepted as the official truth, no matter how false her truth may be. And I was powerless to do anything about it. Because I was homeless. Nobody would believe me.

It was the first moment to break me.

It wouldn't be the last.

Hell's Wrath

The accusations were thrown at me liberally after that moment, by multiple members of staff and volunteers, often in casual remarks made when our paths crossed, veiled as jokey banter. I was repeatedly accused of lying, of alcoholism, of drug addiction, of mental illness and violent anger. Any time I clarified I was neither an alcoholic nor a drug addict, I was told I was in denial. It was part of my sickness. My case worker would pointedly not meet without a "witness" because she feared I would attack her. Often during our sessions, she would announce I was scaring her and leave.

I was starting to experience minor anxiety attacks on a regular basis so started spending as little time as possible there. I felt fine when I was off the premises. I would wake in the morning and take my laptop to a coffee shop, not returning until the curfew at night. Even that was used against me. I was told I had anti-social tendencies, I was refusing to engage, and it was part of the mental health issues I denied having. I was accused of lying about my whereabouts because they had checked the local coffee shop and I hadn't been seen there. Of course I hadn't. It wasn't the coffee shop I frequented. I invited them to speak to the manageress of the shop where I had become a regular client and she could confirm my presence. There was no response. It was one of my few victories. It was small, but I took it. Childishly I stuck out my tongue.

I was repeatedly phoned by staff and volunteers to ask my whereabouts. I was often told to return to attend a meeting, only to have that meeting cancelled after my arrival because something else had come up; or told I was confused –that no meeting had been requested, or had been arranged for another day. I eventually had to turn my phone off because it was sparking anxiety every time it rang. That led to further accusations of anti-social tendencies and paranoia.

One morning I left my room and returned later in the day to discover I had lost my keys. I informed the person at the desk who called one of the members of staff. When he arrived, he announced he wasn't surprised, it was common with people like me. He then asked, "Were you angry? You know what you're like when you're angry. Did you throw them at somebody?" He then laughed and tossed a couple of quick boxer jabs into the air.

I couldn't enter my room because they were –unsurprisingly– too busy to deal with the problem at the time. I would have to wait. I took the time to retrace my steps, even rummaging through a rubbish bin because I remembered throwing out some facial tissue and considered the possibility I had inadvertently dropped my keys in with it. I asked the manageress of the coffee shop who conducted a thorough search of the store with no luck. I returned to Passage House hours later and told them how thoroughly I had looked. I was genuinely apologetic as I knew it would require them to change the lock on my door. I was told my answer sounded "too prepared", accused of lying again, and asked if I was really being honest about losing the keys. I started trembling and the drug accusation was thrown at me again. I was told to wait in the lobby. I asked if I could wait outside and told no, they would only be a few minutes.

Over an hour later one of the case workers returned – the same one who had teased me about my violent anger earlier in the day– and handed me my keys. He said I was lucky he had been able to find them, but I wouldn't have lost them in the first place if it wasn't for my anger. I asked where they had been located and told that wasn't important. I was instead chastised that my first response hadn't been to thank him. I had to learn to be more grateful to people who were trying to help me.

I found out that evening I had simply left them hanging in the lock on my door. One of the other residents on the floor noticed immediately and had come running down after me to return them before I left the building. He had been stopped by the same case worker who had later told me how lucky I was he had found them. The whole afternoon was nothing more than another theatrical performance staged for my benefit.

Another evening I returned and headed straight for the public toilet on my floor, desperate for a bowel movement. As I rushed through the lobby, I heard the worker on the desk phone someone and say, "He's back." While on the toilet, two case workers started banging on the door telling me to open up and forcing me to . . . finish half-way through the movement. They were worried because I looked like I was "tripping". They expressed relief I was fine, then asked if I wanted to discuss my problems with them. More theatrics for the paperwork.

The issue of housing returned with a vengeance. My case worker had located a flat in Plumstead, in Kent. Like a broken record I repeated I could return to my previous residence when I was working and could pay the rent. And I had two potential sources of revenue lined up if they would only allow me to pursue them. I was provided the same roundabout arguments, and told it was impossible to find housing without their help. When I pointed out I had done just that within two weeks of arriving in London, I scored another small victory. There was no response, just a blank stare. I was finally starting to put a few cracks in their facades and enjoyed the feeling immensely. My countering smirk probably should not have been so cocky and smug.

I was then informed I did not meet any of the conditions to be housed in London. This argument had come up before and I had never been provided with the criteria despite asking. I held firm, arguing there may be a requirement they were not aware I met and started listing some potential factors. I had been born there. (*No.*) I was living there at the time I became homeless. (*No.*) I had technically obtained employment there; employment they were preventing me from accepting. (*No – and they weren't preventing me from looking for work.*) I had registered for a course at the City of Westminster College. (*No.*) I asked if my family's history could be a factor. John Kirk had received a knighthood for his philanthropic work in London, and my grandfather had earned an OBE for his work with the British Foreign Office and the British Embassy in Washington D.C. (*No.*). They were dead. I had to have living family members in the city if I wanted to be housed there.

That little nugget of information presented me with a slight moral dilemma.

I did.

I have an older half-sister. Our mother had found herself "in the family way" as a teenager, sent to live with an aunt, and forced to give her first-born child up for adoption. Sadly, they never reunited. My sister was unable to make contact until a few short months after our shared mother passed away. Mere months. Less than half a year. It was devastating, however my father's family picked up the pieces admirably and provided the welcome our mother's family had denied her for decades. You can't choose your family; but when it comes to picking up the pieces, some are better than others.

My sister and I had connected when I arrived in London and made plans to get together once I was firmly on my feet. My subsequent dereliction obviously put a slight dent in those arrangements. She was unable to provide much in the way of assistance as she had pursued a career in the theatre –as an actress and in various behind-the-scenes roles. It is an exciting path, fraught with financial instability. She had navigated the route successfully for decades but was still just getting by. She had neither space nor resources to help her wayward brother.

I hesitated to mention any of it. I had already regretted telling them of my mother's alcoholism as it had had no bearing on my homelessness despite both charities' fixated assertions to the contrary. It wasn't the "root cause" the charity think-tanks love to chant to the media. I was a victim of my own stubbornness more than anything else –an inherited trait to be true, but one my parents had applied more successfully to their lives than I had to mine. They were in no way responsible for my current predicament; the responsibility was mine, and mine alone –something I had willingly acknowledged from the moment I first landed on the streets.

And I was embittered to the interference with my existing family. Relations between my father and I had become understandably strained during this ordeal. During the initial sign-in procedures at both The Connection and Passage House, I had requested he not be contacted, and the relevant box had been ticked. Yet staff at both organizations had made occasional references to conversations held with him. When I asked why they had gone against my wishes, I was informed the agreement I signed gave them the right to discuss my case with anyone they felt was pertinent –in other words, anyone. Nice loophole. When I confronted my father, he at first denied, then admitted to one conversation with my case worker, before asking why I insisted on fighting with them when they were only trying to help. Rightly or wrongly, he lost my trust, and I broke off contact with him for months.

I did not particularly want to add my mother's ancient dirty laundry into the mix, particularly as she was fifteen years' dead and unable to speak for herself. But I was growing increasingly desperate. I needed a lifeline. I wrestled with the integrity behind putting self-interest over family for a few moments –and came up short. I threw my dead mother under the figurative bus and revealed all.

For naught.

I was immediately admonished for not telling them earlier. This was necessary information for my file. I had to tell them everything. Why had I withheld this? What else was I withholding? This was the cause of my mother's alcoholism and the cause of all my problems. They asked for my sister's contact details so they could reach out to her and offer any support. She might need help. Had I not thought of that?

I refused that request point-blank, long having reached the mindset of not wishing charity assistance on my worst enemy, let alone a family member. I asked again if that met the requirement to be housed in London, my only reason for bringing it up.

No. She was only a half-sister. That wasn't a strong enough connection.

Unsurprisingly, that later proved to be another blatant lie.

Though I had not wanted to sign on for Jobseeker's Allowance, it did have a benefit I hadn't taken into consideration at the time. I had to meet with case workers at the Department of Works and Pensions once every three weeks. We had only met a handful of times, but in those few meetings we developed enough of a relationship I felt comfortable enough to start asking questions. It wasn't long before I found myself wishing I had turned to the various government departments relating to my situation instead of the charities when I first found myself lost in the streets of London. The system is not as complicated as I had been led to believe, and the staff not as uncaring as they had been painted. The charities, if anything, are an unnecessary middleman. I soon learned about many of the half-truths and misrepresentations I had been led to believe.

They were also far more understanding of my need to find work quickly, and unsurprised by the charities' resistance to it. I had already attended a few work fairs throughout London and had been signed on to a Work Assistance Program specializing in people over 50 conducted in partnership with Reed's recruitment agency in Willesden, North London. They in turn registered me for a 16-week internship with Lloyd's Bank. I had also registered for a Public Speaking Course through the University of Westminster College. These activities combined with the opportunities presented by Metro and the Casting Connection were all based in the north of London. The flat I was being offered was in Kent, far south of the capital. I was concerned about the length and cost of the commute.

These opportunities combined with the existence of a *half*-sister also met the requirements to be housed in London. I also discovered the government were willing to negotiate with my former landlord –despite the repeated assertions from both charities they would not. I was advised to look at the Plumstead flat and decline it to buy myself time. I had the right to turn down two opportunities, and this was only the first presented by Passage House. The law was on my side.

On Monday17 September 2018 I viewed the flat. In all fairness it had been renovated and was the cleanest I had yet seen. It was remote, there was no place locally where I could acquire regular internet access, and the commute from Kent to North London would have been too lengthy and too costly to afford as there was no local bus or tube service to London. But I was tempted to accept it. I was desperate to leave Passage House; my nerves were rapidly deteriorating. The mere sight of some staff members was enough to instigate a minor anxiety attack. Although I had been advised I could reject it outright, I did want to give it some serious thought before making a decision. The leasing agent was amenable and simply asked for a decision before the end of the week.

My case worker was not. I explained I was considering it but wanted a couple of days to think it over and gave her my reasons. She told me that wasn't allowed. I had to accept now, or I could not stay in the shelter anymore. I told her I had spoken to staff at the Department of Works and Pensions and they had told me they were valid reasons and by law I had the right to turn it down. I also told her they were willing to cover the rent at my previous residence despite my repeatedly being told they wouldn't. Her response was frightening.

"The law doesn't matter! That's our policy!"

She shouted I was the one that had broken the law by speaking to them in the first place. I had breached the confidentiality agreement I had signed in the contract; and I had violated Data Protection Laws. I was now facing serious charges. She again informed me nobody would believe me. I was a liar, and she was going to make sure everybody knew I was a liar. She then screamed at me to get out. I ran.

I returned that night and was surprised to be allowed back in. At that point I concluded she was bluffing and decided to call her on it. When I returned the next night, Tuesday, 18 September, there was a letter on my bed claiming my reason for rejecting the flat was invalid and if I didn't accept by Thursday, 20 September, I would be banned from Passage House for 24 hours, and would have to accept the flat or I would not be allowed to return. I held firm.

When I returned Wednesday, 19 September, I was denied entry. I argued their own letter stated the ban wouldn't be put into effect until the next night and was told it didn't matter. I asked if I could grab my sleeping bag and a sweater. No; it was part of the ban. I had also been allowing my 'Partner in Crime' to store his sleeping bag and possessions in my room during the day and asked if I could retrieve them. Again no.

Suffice to say, he was not pleased. We returned ten minutes later and were denied entry. We stood on the front step for a few moments until one of the other residents left the building, politely holding the door open for us.

All hell broke loose.

We burst into the front lobby and he told me to get our stuff. I raced up the four flights of stairs to my room to the sound of shouts and yells from below. One of the staff chased after me shouting at me to stop or they would call the police. I entered my room and only had the opportunity to grab my mate's possessions that were lying within easy reach on my bed before my pursuer caught up with me screaming at me to get out, they were calling the police. I was petrified. I was escorted downstairs and we were both escorted out of the building. We didn't even make it to the end of the road before we burst out laughing. It had been frightening, but it had been strangely fun.

I returned the next morning and was again denied entry because my case worker was not on duty. I would have to wait until she started her shift. I asked when that was and told they couldn't tell me. I asked if she was even working that day and again told I could not be given that information. I asked if I could just change clothes and grab a couple of possessions –particularly my laptop, and told I was too great a security risk. I wandered the streets for hours, returned in the afternoon, denied entry again, and wandered a few hours more.

When I returned that evening, I was exhausted, hungry, and willing to agree to anything. I rang the bell and after a few minutes my case worker opened the door a crack. She asked if I was on drugs. I answered no. I asked if I could please come in. She said no; I had made my choice. I asked if I could grab some of my possessions." No." I asked if someone could gather a few things for me, willing to allow them entry to my room. "No."

I burst into tears and started begging, repeating "Please" and "I'm sorry" in increasingly breathless gulps. She said she would think about it and closed the door. I sat on the steps snivelling, weeping, the phlegm pouring from my nose, mixing with my tears, and running down my face, into my mouth, and onto my clothes. I didn't even have a tissue to wipe it away. I used my sleeves and my hands, but eventually they become too wet and sticky themselves to be of any use.

The crying eventually subsided and after half an hour she stepped outside, closing the door behind her. She said I could only be allowed back inside if I agreed to accept the flat. Barely able to muster a whisper I made a final, weak attempt to stand up for myself. I told her that was blackmail. It was wrong. She said "It doesn't matter. Nobody cares." The tears started flowing again and I accepted.

Only to have the rug yanked out from under me one last time. It was too late. The flat had been taken. I had screwed everything up. They had tried to help me, and I had screwed it up. I couldn't come back because I couldn't be helped. Nobody could help me. I was too sick. I needed to be locked up.

That was the second incident to break me. Another piece of my psyche broke away and shattered on the steps beneath us, but with a different reaction. Not the silent numbing horror that had overtaken me before, it was quick and explosive. A stabbing pain engulfed my head, matched by another in my chest. I fell back against the railing, grabbed my head in my hands, and started shouting "Stop it! Stop it! Sto—o-o . . ..!" My words vanishing into a long, high-pitched scream that blinded me. My eyes were wide open and flowing with tears, but I saw only whiteness. I began punching myself in the head repeatedly with my right hand. The world lost all form. My body lost all form. Past, present and future lost all form. For those few moments existence as I knew it consisted of nothing more than that scream: a shrill, blood-curdling, eternal scream.

To any passers-by walking to or from the pubs, take-away restaurants, and shops that were within screaming distance I looked like just another addict having a seizure on the steps of Passage House. It was a common occurrence, and a reasonable conclusion to draw. I had drawn the same conclusion myself when I witnessed similar episodes in the past. One of the residents would suffer a seizure while a member of staff looked impassively on, quietly waiting for the frenzy to end. It was Passage House, a temporary shelter for drug addicts. The whole community was accustomed to the bedlam. I was just another junkie, providing some temporary real-life entertainment for the locals. A horrific and unwilling theatrical performance with me as the star: great optics in favour of the poor, long-suffering staff.

The scream ended. My body and the surrounding world regained their corporeal forms. I leaned against the railing, heaving, shaking, docile and compliant, looking to her for help, my eyes pleading for even the smallest sign of sympathy.

Silly me.

She asked if I had learned my lesson. "Yes." She said she didn't hear me and made me repeat it. She made me say it aloud in full: "Yes. I have learned my lesson." She asked me if I was ready to admit I needed help. I agreed. She made me repeat that as well: "Yes; I need help." I vaguely understood she was turning the screws but was too weak and too frightened to do anything about it. I was too shattered to do anything but agree.

"Good," she said. Her look softened. She even smiled. She told me I was lucky. She felt sorry for me. No-one else did. I was lucky she was still trying to help me despite my fighting her all the time. She said it was bending the rules to allow me back in, but if I promised to accept the next flat she found, she would let me return. I agreed. She asked if there was anything I wanted to say to her, and I provided the answer she was looking for, hating both her and myself as the words left my lips:

"Thank you."

Hell's Saviour

It was my only real attempt at suicide. I had flirted with the idea with varying levels of commitment. I had even threatened it in desperate attempts to get someone, anyone to step in and rescue me, or to convince the staff to end their mistreatment even if only to buy myself a temporary reprieve. It would work, and I would be left to my own devices for a few days, but ultimately it only served to add more fodder to my increasingly unflattering case files. This was my only serious effort. No drama, no warning, no last-minute cry for help. I simply woke up and started preparing for it like a normal everyday event.

I had been sent to the Borough of Brent a week after leaving my second consignment of psyche debris shattered on the front steps of Passage House. My case worker had taken the rare step of reverting to Jekyll form and affably told me she had taken my request to be housed north of London seriously and had gone to great lengths to find a place. It hadn't been easy, and she had had to work on her own time to arrange it. She was friendly and pleasant in demeanour, but Hyde still dwelt in her eyes when she reminded me I had agreed to accept it.

I made the journey, and it proved the worst of all the viewings I had attended, not only for myself, but with friends I had accompanied on their prospective housing assignments. The front yard was rubble, littered with beer cans, drug paraphernalia and smashed bottles. The wheelie bin used for recycling lay on its side, melted and ripped apart. One front window was smashed: the other boarded up with plywood. The stench of urine in the entry hall was so strong both the leasing agent and I gagged and covered our mouths until we grew accustomed to it. The overhead light had been broken and was hanging from the socket by its connecting wires. There were broken steps in the staircase leading to the next level, and the banister had been snapped off the wall. There were holes in the downstairs wall that were presumably made by fists, and darkish streaks of something I could not readily identify. The torn notices referring to a previous tenant's arrest for violent assault and informing the residents that "excessive partying, fights, weapons and drugs would result in immediate arrest and full prosecution," provided a queasy suggestion as to the identity of the streaks.

The room itself was not bad, larger than most I had previously viewed. It was dark because the electricity supply had been suspended, and thick with dust. It was spacious enough to accommodate not only a bed and dresser, but a table and chair –a rarity. There was a door leading to the backyard that looked newly installed, but the backyard itself looked as apocalyptically appealing as the front. I genuinely questioned how long I would survive living there.

My phone rang. It was my case worker. She asked what I thought. I couldn't think of a single word in response. "Well?" she asked? I started to describe the surroundings, but she cut me off, told me it didn't matter. I had made a promise. She disconnected. I signed the agreement.

I was quiet for the next two days, lost in the fog of depression, keeping to myself as much as possible. When friends asked if I was alright, I told them I was fine, just tired. When I woke up the third morning, I had no specific thought to end my life, but proceeded to take the required steps like an automaton programmed for death. I purchased a bottle of Jack Daniel's whiskey and four Stella Artois beers from the local Sainsbury's. I went to three separate pharmacists and purchased a wide selection of over-the-counter medications for whatever cocktail I would ultimately blend. I had no plans to leave a note or give any indication of my purpose. I simply intended to quietly slip away … to quietly slip away.

I knew exactly where I would spend my final moments, and where I would be found. One of my first accomplishments after arriving in London was to locate Sir John Kirk's grave. His 'celebrity' at the time of his death in 1922 was so great its location was never revealed to prevent the hordes of expected mourners from wreaking unintentional mayhem at the site. I had reasoned it would likely be within walking distance of his final residence for his widow –well into her 70s– to visit. That address was a small house called 'Tanglewood' in Dorking. I had located the house, spotted a nearby church steeple and sure enough, there he lay. As Sir John had been the reason for my coming to England, it seemed appropriate to complete my departure at his gravesite.

Leaving unnoticed proved impossible and I found myself joining a group of friends passing the day in front of Westminster Cathedral. I put on a little theatrical performance of my own, engaging in the jokey banter seemingly without a care in the world. I smiled. I laughed. I was the living embodiment of normal. Nothing to see here. Everything is normal.

Too normal. And my laughter was not. I have a distinctive 'love it or hate it' laugh that cannot be faked no matter how hard I try, particularly when someone knows me. My 'Partner in Crime' loved it, saying it reminded him of the killer doll from the "Child's Play" movies. He dubbed me 'Chucky' on our first meeting and that was forever the name I was known by within the homeless communities of Charing Cross and Westminster, strangely adding to my street credibility. Better to share a name with a homicidal doll than a paedophile. He picked up on the lie in my laugh, saw through my act, and when I said my 'normal' "See you later" good-byes, quietly followed me.

As lovely as it would be to share an intense Shakespearean account of two middle-aged men pondering the uncertainties of life and death in an English village grave-yard, spouting lyrical soliloquys with skulls raised to the heavens in the palms of our hands; the reality was emphatically mundane. Real life generally is, no matter how dramatic the circumstances.

My journey to the afterlife was set to begin on a double-decker bus, the first of three to take me to Dorking. Realizing he could no longer follow me without revealing himself, he sauntered up out of the blue and asked, "What's up, Chuck?"

"Nothing. Fuck off."

"Uh-huh." He reached for the rucksack at my feet, opened it, and pulled out the four cans of beer. "Uh-huh," he repeated. He cracked one open, handed it to me, cracked open a second and began drinking it himself. "What you up to?"

"Nothing. Fuck off."

"Uh-huh."

Hardly the "To be or not to be" melodrama of Hamlet. My life was saved drinking beer on the red plastic bench at a transit shelter for the 148 bus to Shepherd's Green, my personal Gateway to Eternity. Sorry Shakespeare.

We spent the rest of the day talking, eventually making our way to St. James Park, stopping only to pick up more beer and a couple of loaves of bread to feed the ducks. He did most of the talking. I had shifted from suicide to sulk mode and was happy to stay there. He shared details from his past, including his own suicide attempt a few years previously. He admitted my situation looked dark but had faced darkness himself and learned to stare it down. He said no matter how bad things get, no matter how much people fuck you over, never give them the satisfaction of killing yourself. Go down fighting and make them take you down. And give 'em the fucking finger when they do it.

He also shared the coping mechanisms he had learned in prison. Anger management techniques and methods to fight depression. He recommended I join his gym not only to put on some sorely needed weight, but to release the negative energy as loud and as violent as I wanted. And he told me never to lose my laugh. It was my best weapon. It made others laugh. It helped others. It helped him. Let them take my life, but never let them take my laugh.

We drank some more, and while feeding the ducks he asked where I was going when he caught up with me. When I told him, he stared at me with complete bewilderment and exclaimed, "*Dorking*?! Jesus, Chuck. I can think of better places to kill myself. The fuck is wrong with you?"

I had to laugh.

We made our way to Trafalgar Square and spent the evening perched on the National Gallery wall heckling the buskers with other homeless friends. That day was my lowest moment, but one of his finest hours. He had not only pulled me from the brink of suicide, he had planted the seeds I needed to survive. An education far more valuable than any taught in school. They had little immediate effect but stayed rooted in the back of my mind and slowly spread. Lessons I later discovered were not only important for survival, but in the healing that comes after the battle has been won or lost. Street wisdom I will continue to live by until that fateful day, long in the future, when I finally shuffle off this mortal coil.

I couldn't have asked for a better friend. Had he not eventually been convinced by other friends on the street to stop taking the medication he needed so he could drink and smoke weed with them; had he not been so mistreated by the charities he had turned to for help after his release from prison and his legitimate desire to reform, later events may not have transpired as they did. His story is far more tragic than mine. But it is not my story to tell. I'm a human being —not a fund-raiser or social justice warrior seeking to exploit the stories of others to further a great and glorious cause. His story is his and his alone to tell, wherever the streets have taken him.

Stories like his need to be heard.

Hell's Victory

Resolving to go down fighting is admirable in theory, but not so easy to commit to when you are nearing the end of a losing battle. Nursing a vicious hangover, I spent the next day gathering the paperwork I needed for my new landlord: proof of identity, proof of previous address, proof of benefits, National Insurance Number, and bank statements for the previous three months. Two days after that, I was sent to sign the final paperwork to move into my new home.

I was accompanied by one of the Passage House staff –one of their Jekylls, everyone's friend, trusted by no-one. I presumed after my eleventh-hour save in the offices of Assisted Accommodation I wasn't trusted to follow through. We arrived early and found ourselves waiting in uncomfortable silence together for two hours past the appointed time. When we finally met with the leasing agent, he started scrutinizing my bank statements asking questions about every withdrawal and deposit listed. What had I withdrawn this £20 for? What had I purchased at this supermarket? What had I spent that amount on at this coffee shop? It seemed a lot to spend for a coffee.

He poured over the deposits with the same micro-
scopic study. My Jobseekers Allowance payments were
straightforward, but he noticed the deposit made when
my friend in Toronto had lent me money on my arrival at
The Connection, and another made by my aunt within
the past month. He asked why those deposits had been
made. He then told me I would have to provide *their* bank
details before we could proceed with the lease. I asked
why. He answered he needed the guarantee he could still
collect rent if I defaulted. I told him that was ridiculous;
illegal; and he *had* that guarantee: the government is paying. He replied I shouldn't be accepting money while
collecting benefits as that constitutes fraud. He said far
too many people used the charities, "took advantage of
their kindness", to defraud the system. "I don't know
how they do things in Canada, but we take that very seriously here." He asked my chaperone if he was aware of
these payments who answered in the negative.

I couldn't speak. I tried but was completely incapable
of talking. The good old, always reliable tremors kicked
into gear and I quietly started crying. He said, "You're
shaking. Are you on drugs?" I couldn't respond. I cannot
clarify how much time elapsed while the three of us sat
in silence as they watched the tears slowly trickle down
my face –probably not much, but it felt like hours. Pure
silence as they watched me cry, punctuated by an occasional sniff as I tried to prevent my nose from running.

My chaperone suddenly put a hand on my shoulder
and said, "I'll take care of this." He left the room to make
a phone call and I sat there, still weeping, still sniffing,

alone with the leasing agent who just sat there and watched. After a few minutes my chaperone returned, assuring me it was all right. I had been given permission to turn down the flat. I was still moderately catatonic as we left, but as we were walking out the door clearly saw him turn to the agent and say, "Thanks. This won't be a problem now. We'll be in touch," and give him a thumbs up.

I spent the duration of our return to Passage House listening to my chaperone tell me how lucky it was he had been there to help me "dodge a bullet." I was reminded of this heroic rescue for days afterward by all the staff, accompanied by the now familiar refrains they were only trying to help, I should be grateful, and they were the only ones who cared about my well-being.

I was extremely sceptical of the entire rescue itself, suspecting it had been yet another theatrical performance staged for my benefit. One that had wasted my second choice for accommodation. But I hoped to take advantage of the reprieve to return to my previous flat. I had been in touch with the landlords and they were open to the idea. I was going to provide their contact details to the Department of Works and Pensions at our next meeting.

I explained this to my case worker when we met to discuss my final housing option. After reminding me yet again they had helped me "dodge a bullet", she explained it was the only accommodation available in North London and I would have to accept a flat in the south. I needed to get over my obsession with living in London. I reminded her it was to take advantage of the employment and training opportunities I had arranged. I told her of the plans I was organizing, and she said I couldn't make my own housing arrangements without them. I told her that was not true as I was in the process of doing just that. She reminded me I had breached confidentiality and data protection laws and could face prosecution. I told her I didn't care; I was doing it anyway. She then said I could only accept if it went through Passage House and asked for my former landlord's contact details. I refused. She told me I was pushing my luck. I repeated, "I don't care." The meeting came to a chilly close.

A few days later my former landlord phoned me. He told me the charity had been in touch and he had decided not to go ahead with the arrangements. He wasn't aware of my issues and had to think of the safety of his other tenants. He wished me luck and disconnected. I quietly cried myself to sleep that night and the next, stifling my chokes and sobs any time I heard the familiar sound of footsteps in the hall outside my room.

An unexpected and unrelated ray of light soon pierced through the gloom, connected to the biography that had inspired me to come to England in the first place. Throughout my stay at Passage House I was repeatedly pressed to get involved in their history project, as I had been at The Connection. I heard the familiar reminder that I could use my skills to write for them, with the new admonition that I was selfish for not wanting to share my talent with others. I generally rolled my eyes and ignored it, but an opportunity was being presented that genuinely attracted my interest.

The staff of Passage House had organized a tour of Buckingham Palace for their residents. As John Kirk had received a knighthood there in 1907, and my grandfather, Frank Mitchell, had received an OBE from Queen Elizabeth in 1963, I was keen to visit the same room where the honours are bestowed. It was a strong connection to my family's history -twice over. I eagerly signed up and was genuinely excited. I even agreed to write about the occasion when prodded.

It proved even better than hoped. The woman who currently organizes these events accompanied us. After explaining the family history, we spent most of the tour with our heads bent in conversation. She agreed to exchange contact details so she could arrange a private visit and grant me access to their archives to find material relating to both ancestors and their communications with the Palace. It was a once-in-a-lifetime opportunity and I was chomping at the bit to grasp it.

When I sought her out at the end of the tour her demeanour had changed entirely. She looked wary, nervous and uncomfortable in my presence. I asked to exchange emails and she said she had been speaking to the Passage House member who had arranged the tour and to discuss it with him. She then told me she hoped I get the help I needed before hurrying away, eager to leave me behind.

I immediately asked the relevant case worker. He said this was not the time or place. We were in Buckingham Palace and it was not the place to create a scene. He would give me the contact details another day after we had a meeting to discuss it. I asked to arrange a meeting right away. He said "Not now. Later," and told me to stop harassing him.

One of the other Passage House residents on the tour joked, "You know you're never going to get those details." I agreed, but still tried. I tried three times to arrange a meeting and received the default charity reply of "Too busy." Every time I was told I had to fill in a Customer Satisfaction Survey about my stay at Passage House before we could discuss it. I would also be asked when I was going to write about the tour for them. I told them I was "Too busy."

It was bad enough they were using my immediate family as pawns to either explain the "root cause" of my issues and homelessness, or to wield as carrots or weapons to induce my compliance on any given day. They were now ransacking my family's history. It was an area they had no right to intrude on as it had nothing to do with how I fell into my circumstances, or how I would climb out of them. Nothing was sacred. Nothing *is* sacred in the obsessive charity drive for data on their clients.

My 'zombification' began then; and would benumb me with varying degrees of intensity throughout the following year. I simply gave up. I was coherent, functional, and in full possession of my mental faculties; but I lost all capacity for emotion. No anger. No gloom. No grief or sorrow. I was nothing more than a husk shambling through the motions of existence. I had committed to life –that surprisingly remained unchanged– but I was too exhausted and weak to commit to going down with a fight.

Sure enough, my dead grandfather became the carrot of choice. They had overheard during my Palace conversation that his career had started as a Councillor for South Croydon in the 1930s. That was suddenly a fitting criteria for housing despite my previously being told otherwise. I didn't care. They knew of an available flat in Selsdon and had started making the necessary arrangements as I had to agree to accept it anyway. I didn't care. I was admonished for not sharing this information with them at the start because if I had, all this unpleasantness would have been avoided. Despite all the drama I had created they were pleased they had found a happy ending to my homelessness; living where my grandparents had once lived. I was lucky they had persevered. I should be pleased, and –as always–I should be grateful. I didn't have to fight the urge to vomit on them. I simply didn't care anymore. I accepted the flat.

I met with the leasing agency on October 30th and signed the contract, accepting a flat at a rent almost twice what I had been paying at my previous accommodation. When I returned to Passage House, they announced I would be moving in that night. I hastily packed my belongings and waited in the lobby while they arranged a taxi to take me to Selsdon. The cab arrived shortly after 9:00 p.m. As I was loading my belongings, the staff on duty informed me there was a phone call for me in the lobby, but to make it quick as the taxi was waiting, and they were paying for it.

It was Crisis. I was surprised because I had not had any contact with them for three months after being told they couldn't interfere with the work of other charities. She asked me about "the status of my situation." I asked if I could phone her back the next day as it wasn't a good time. I had a taxi waiting. She said, "So they've found you a place?" When I hesitatingly answered in the affirmative, she cut me short and gushed, "Great. So it's a happy ending then," and disconnected. I was promptly bundled off in the cab.

My "happy ending" began when I arrived at the flat shortly after 10:30 that night. There was no electricity in my room. No lights. No heat. The meter indicated it was over £30 in arrears. The door from my room leading into the back yard had no lock. There was also no bed. No stores were open at that time of night to do anything about it. And two of the other tenants were drinking up a storm with the stereo blazing in the room down the hall. I unrolled my sleeping bag, unpacked my clothes to use as a makeshift blanket for additional warmth, and spent the night shivering and staring into the darkness.

My phone ran out of power during the night, and without electricity I had no way to charge the battery. I also couldn't use the shower as it was connected to the electric water heater and wouldn't run hot or cold. I had only £40 in my bank account, and because the Universal Credit benefits system makes payments a month in arrears, that had to last from October 31st to December 2nd. Happy ending indeed.

A new bed was delivered the following day. The landlords hadn't expected me to move in that same night and were genuinely apologetic. It took four days to arrange the electricity, two of those days spent travelling around London trying to obtain the correct pre-payment key for the meter, eating up over £10 of my funds. The arrears were cleared as they were not my responsibility, and I spent another £10 charging the key so I could turn the electricity on. I had less than £20 to stretch over a month.

I spent an additional £4.50 travelling to the Marylebone Job Centre to arrange the transfer of my account to their location in Purley. I explained the financial disaster, and they quietly provided a much-needed lifeline. I was not only switching offices; I was transferring from an old benefits system to the Universal Credit model in the early stages of its launch. I was only due two days of Jobseeker's allowance before my transfer. I received the full two-week payment. This error was corrected the next month, leaving me with just under £200 per month to survive on for the first two months. But it was enough. I spent that Christmas without heat, and barely eating enough to subsist on, but it guaranteed survival that otherwise would not have been possible.

Sadly, it was not enough money to take advantage of the job opportunities I had arranged. I had to drop out of the 16-week internship with Lloyd's Bank because I could not afford the cost of daily transportation to northern London with the austere amount of cash available. For similar reasons I had to turn down opportunities presented by the Casting Connection. And my 'zombification' impeded my ability to write, to provide features for the Metro website. I would try, and each attempt would be tearfully abandoned as I discovered that part of my brain had shut down and remained inaccessible. I was too tired, too defeated, too burnt-out.

I would soon discover the other four tenants had been placed there by Crisis. The property itself was well known throughout the neighbourhood as the Crisis house where they arranged tenancies for their clients. For an organization that professed not to interfere with the work of other charities, they did a lot to help them behind the scenes, whether those actions were in the best interest of the people they were helping or not.

My charity organised "happy ending" came with one final, unexpected surprise. A month after moving in, I noticed a peculiar visitor on my LinkedIn social media account: James S., a private investigator who conducted investigations for various government departments in England. I had connections with less than 10 people at that point, all in Canada, so thought the chance of anyone randomly landing on my profile were slim –particularly when he visited over a succeeding number of days.

I asked my new case worker if it had anything to do with my benefits. He didn't respond, simply stared at his computer screen for a few moments before changing the topic. I asked through my online Universal Credit journal repeatedly over the next month with no response. Finally, after more than a month I was informed the private investigator had nothing to do with their department.

That turned out to be yet another lie.

At the end of January I received an official letter from the Department of Works and Pensions informing me an investigation *had been conducted* based on an anonymous tip I had refused to search for or accept employment from May to November of 2018, the exact length of time I spent with The Connection and Passage House, fighting them tooth and nail over the employment issue. The investigation had concluded I was not guilty of wrong-doing and there would be no interruption to my benefits, and I would not be subject to any penalties or charges.

I had no way to discover the identity of the anonymous complainant, but the message had come through loud and clear, as it had since the first day The Connection's big red door closed behind me.

Help the charities . . . or fuck you.

My two-year deadline expired. I lost my Permanent Resident status. I could no longer return to Canada. I could no longer return home.

There's No Place Like Housing

Welcome to your new home. Your 'charity approved' home. The housing your charity, and others like them, promote as the successful resolution to your homeless odyssey. The happily ever after they endorse far and wide through the media and their own fund-raising campaigns. Your new life. Your better life. The life they reckon you deserve. Welcome to your reckoning.

Time and money become your mortal enemies. A dearth of pennies, an overabundance of minutes –they unite to slowly weaken you. You can't afford to go out. You can't afford to stay in. You can't afford to work. You can't afford to relax. The amount of mental energy consumed by stretching the pennies while filling the minutes is staggering. It is constant. It is exhausting. You set financial targets no-one truly has a chance of achieving under the circumstances, and steel yourself while the minutes slowly drag you down. Though theoretically possible, the reality prevents you from achieving these almost laughable penny-pinching goals. When you invariably fail to reach them, you mentally beat yourself up for that failure because they were technically attainable. That guilt, that self-flagellation adds more fuel to the already unbearable daily pressure of filling time.

You conduct a lot of trial and error research, and the errors are costly. Oh, so costly. The margin of error for mistakes is non-existent. Because mis-spent pennies add up quickly. Spilling milk at the wrong time of the month is a financial catastrophe. You don't cry; you chastise yourself for your clumsiness. And the continual self-recrimination over this and other gaffes that would be nothing more than trivial hiccups under normal living conditions adds to the already exhausting task of getting through the day. Poverty is *not* a normal living condition, but you make do the best you can.

You grow accustomed to the dry cereal for breakfast. The ketchup sandwiches for lunch. The toasted ketchup sandwiches when the bread has surpassed its expiry date and you need to tear off the green bits in order to eat it. The one-cup tea bags stretched out to four. (After the fourth cup you're just drinking bitter water.) The single can of vegetables or half cups of rice for dinner. Butter is a luxury you quickly abandon. Meat is a luxury you quickly abandon. Fulfilling your daily nutritional requirements – a luxury you quickly abandon. You suffer through one day of fasting per week, and regularly make the effort to suffer through two.

It grows easier as your stomach shrinks, your weight drops, and your body requires less food to sustain itself. You are literally wasting away, but it proves cost-effective, so you accept the physical deterioration as a blessing, not a burden. Every pound lost is a penny saved.

You space your showers out to every other day, then every second day, sometimes even a third, so you can save the pennies consumed by the electricity required to heat the water. Shaving becomes a once-a-week ritual you eventually abandon as another luxury you cannot afford. You change your underwear twice a week, then dispense with wearing it altogether because it is an unnecessary piece of clothing. You wash your clothes in the sink with dishwashing liquid. You wash your face and hands with dishwashing liquid. You wash your hair with dishwashing liquid. Just add water. And keep adding water to avoid replacing it as long as possible. You carefully separate your toilet paper along its perforated allowances, then painstakingly tear it in half again. You try to tear it in quarters, but it proves unpleasantly unworkable. Trial and error.

As the weeks stretch endlessly on you put off the most basic of tasks in order to have something to do later. If you clean in the morning you have nothing to do to fill the afternoon. By the time afternoon rolls around the evening's emptiness hovers in your thoughts. And as the evening slowly ticks by you cheer yourself with the thought that holding off your chores will give you something to fill your day tomorrow. So you put them off. And put them off. And put them off. Over time the natural sluggishness that develops from doing nothing kicks in and you eventually lack the energy needed to complete the simplest of tasks. And when your living space is so

modest removing your shoes makes the room look un-
naturally cluttered, you lose heart at the Sisyphean
futility of it all anyway. Comfort is a luxury you cannot
afford.

When there is no conceivable space to place a chair, let
alone a small table or desk without adding to the already
crushing claustrophobia of your room, you have no
choice but to conduct the daily mechanics of living on
your bed: sleeping, eating, reading, counting the minutes
that have yet to be filled, counting the pennies you can't
afford to spend, staring at the spiders as they weave their
webs in the corners of the ceiling, commiserating with the
flies as they become ensnared in their final home to await
their looming deaths. You appreciate their futility and
watch their struggles to escape with dispassionate indifference.

Spiders and flies are not the only visitors to grace my
humble home with their presence. There are also snails.
How they get in I have never worked out. The back door
leading out of my room has no lock, but it has a handle
to turn in order to gain entry. I remember a cat we owned
when I was growing up in Canada, Tigger, who had fig-
ured out how to open the outside door after weeks of
patient feline study. A single leap, some determined
wrestling and voila! Freedom to rut in the streets as all
self-respecting cats do. She later gave birth to four ador-
able kittens, beginning the process on top of me while I
was asleep in bed. After the on-the-spot "birds and bees"
talk valiantly delivered by my mother who had been
woken by my screams, Tigger, previously thought to be

male, was thereafter called Miss Tiggy and sent for a little operation that resulted in yet another awkward life lesson at the feet of my poor, grossly underappreciated mother. Those are the memories the charities can't taint, can't poison, can't take away from you.

But opening a door is a feat I am still reasonably certain snails lack the intellectual capacity, let alone the manual dexterity to accomplish. But enter they do, uninvited and slimily unpleasant, especially when you inadvertently step on one with your bare foot and hear the sickening crunch of its shell as its shattered fragments pierce your foot. I regularly stock up on salt to remove the snails from those ubiquitous "hard to reach" places. They are relentless.

Still, they are company for the spiders. Maybe the spiders are letting them in. Who knows? I have never been able to figure it out: a mystery of life as perplexing as the Bermuda Triangle, Bigfoot, and the socks that go missing from the tumble dryer. Maybe the snails are stealing our socks. Who knows?

As for the horrors of the communal kitchen? I don't use it. Its temporary closure due to the risk of e-coli infection from an infestation of maggots the summer after I was forced into tenancy validated that little decision above and beyond all reasonable doubt. They were cooking for the snails presumably. Spiders and maggots and snails –oh my. Home sweet bloody home.

The revulsion doesn't end there. When you live in one of five tiny, self-contained rooms that have been converted from a former single family dwelling, you slowly develop a scientific knowledge related to the odours emitted by the faeces of your fellow tenants as they waft through the pipes into your miniscule "en suite". You become privy to their eating habits without ever seeing them put food in their mouths. You learn to differentiate between the smoky acrid scent of charcoal and the sickly, gag-inducing stench of rotten eggs. You begin to fear the occasional unrecognizable aromas that are beyond your knowledge, but just as unpleasant.

The roar of flushing from Flat Four makes my heart sink more than all the other flats combined. He obviously isn't healthy, and I fear possible unseen contagion spreading into my room in the very air I breath. I tried shutting the door to my bathroom with some success, but it takes hours to dissipate, and I find myself unable to relieve my own bodily functions without fighting the urge to vomit at the same time. I would open my back door to allow fresh air to enter the room, but it also gives the worst of the seasons' elements –rain, snow, heat, cold– unfiltered access. It is all but impossible to escape.

On the bright side it made the cost-saving decision to ration showers that much easier to bear. You search for silver linings wherever you can find them, even in the shit of others.

Escape, even temporary, is virtually impossible. The reality of your lodging follows you wherever you go. Shopping expeditions consist of popping into coffee houses and asking the baristas for permission to use their facilities without making the required purchase, then using the opportunity to surreptitiously pocket their sugar, condiments, napkins, and toilet paper. If you're lucky you find a replacement roll perched on the tank you easily whisk into your rucksack before making your polite escape. More often than not you find yourself sitting on the defecatory throne slowly unravelling long swaths of perforated sheets and meticulously folding them to hide in your pocket with a minimum of tearing. Toilet paper serves multiple purposes, so you never waste money on facial tissue or paper towels. When the formerly sympathetic baristas grow suspicious of your thievery and understandably put an end to your weekly visits, you swallow the embarrassment, shrug defiantly, and move on to the next café.

My conscience had weakened considerably over two years, enough to allow my transformation into the Al Capone of Condiments; but it would still not allow me to cross the threshold into outright theft. I would take gratuitous advantage of the free peripherals surrounding a purchase, but I would not steal a purchased product itself. It was weakening, but my conscience was still waging an ambitious fight.

Not that it mattered.

Once I had been identified as a tenant of *"that* house", the local Costa Coffee Franchise refused to serve me after my third visit. I hadn't been stealing *their* condiments under the unspoken rule you don't create messes in your own backyard. It didn't matter. The local grapevine had informed the franchise owner I was a resident of *"that* house" and I was automatically approved for the same banishment served to the other tenants of my humble home. I vowed to stop supporting all shops in the Costa chain from that point forward. I wouldn't even lower myself to pilfer their condiments and toilet paper –a pyrrhic retaliation admittedly, and drenched in hypocrisy, but it was the only weapon I had.

The community whispers also reached the local Sainsbury's supermarket, and I soon found myself accompanied by bored security guards 'discretely' following me from aisle to aisle, muttering to their colleagues through their radios. I couldn't use the automated self-serve checkouts without a staff member hovering to ensure I didn't use the opportunity to slip a five-fingered discount into my pocket or help myself to a plastic carrier bag without charging myself the obligatory 20 pence fee. One time I was even searched by two security guards and a store manager –had my shopping emptied item by item to be checked for the corresponding entry on the receipt. There was no theft to uncover, I had even paid the 20 pence for the plastic shopping bag. Their mandatory apology after the public embarrassment was provided with the same dry insincerity as my acceptance of it.

Even standing outside to smoke a cigarette to take advantage of their free customer wi-fi access to check emails and social media messages from Canada invariably led to a security guard coming outside and asking me to move along, or simply lean against the railing and stare directly at me. I had grown used to this treatment when I had been living on the streets but had assumed it would end when I was respectably housed. Silly me.

Social housing is wonderful in theory, but the surrounding businesses and residents are more than vigilant in reminding you social housing residents are *not* socially acceptable; are *not* welcome; and are *not* wanted. Putting humiliation aside, it gets on your nerves. I found myself toying with the idea of stealing –not from need or hunger like Jean Valjean with his nobly appropriated loaf of bread– but out of pure spite. A symbolic middle finger thrust in the faces of my false accusers. I have come close to doing it many times, too many times for comfort. Morality is a twisted referee.

Because the uncomfortable truth I can only admit to myself in the barest of whispers? I don't blame them. I live in "*that* house". "*That* house" you can identify not by number, but by the overgrown weeds, soiled mattress, drug paraphernalia and beer cans littering the front lawn. "*That* house" that serves as a regular stopping place for other addicts and their drug dealers; for police cars and ambulances; for parties, fights and chaos that often spills into the streets –usually in the small hours of the morning when the neighbourhood is trying to sleep. "*That* house" that gives birth to the vandalism, theft, and violence that plagues the surrounding businesses and properties. "*That* house" the community knows to be Crisis' 'charity approved' holding pen for addicts. "*That* house" the community rightfully despises.

And I don't blame them. I despise it myself. And feel ashamed for being associated with it. Ashamed for living there. Ashamed for living. All I can do is grit my teeth, thicken my skin and broaden my shoulders to bear the weight of the scorn and shame as I conduct my necessary business outside my room. And when I return I can only lie in bed, avoiding the snails, avoiding the housemates, and watching the spiderwebs to avoid thinking of the infinite minutes that stretch out before me all day, every day, every week, every month, every year. And flinch when the periodical flushing from Flat Four brings the olfactory reminder that even the very air I breathe is at the defecatory mercy of others. It is existential suffering at its most banal.

This is the life you enter when placed in 'charity approved' housing. These are the living conditions the charities promote as the "Successful Resolution" to all your homeless woes. Another happy tick for their books; another success story to promote in their endless fundraising campaigns. This is the solution the charities demand the government make easier to provide, and campaign for legislation to force all property owners to accept. No charity worker or volunteer will open their own home to the Tribe of the Homeless –and understandably so– but they are more than willing to chastise other property owners for sharing the same understandable fears and concerns. It is self-righteous finger-pointing hypocrisy of the highest degree.

These are not sheltered sanctuaries from the dangers of the streets. These are holding pens for charities to shelve their processed clients, often throwing alcoholics and addicts together in a single house to succumb to their chemical dependencies hand in hand in a freefall of enablement. This is not a step to independence, for the conditions make it virtually impossible to obtain employment, let alone keep it for any length of time. Whether intentional or not, the tenants are simply set-up for failure. Many do, and find themselves falling deeper into their addictions, falling back onto the streets, and calling on the charities that put them there to pick up the pieces again. You don't need a career in business journalism to know the best customer is a repeat customer.

This is not Happily Ever After Housing. This is homelessness with a roof.

This is not successful resolution.

This is erosion of the soul.

Rude Awakenings from Sleeping Rough

I woke up in St. James Park this morning to find a man masturbating over me while I slept.

Bizarrely, my first reaction was "Thank God it's not a cop." The harsh reality of what I had woken to quickly became evident; but by that point the pervert had tucked himself back into his track-pants and was running away.

The incident didn't end there.

Realizing my day was starting at 3:50 a.m. I gathered myself together and was disgusted to find the top of my jeans and bottom of my shirt were damp with his pre-ejaculation discharge. The smell was easily masked with the aerosol deodorant in my rucksack, but the dampness and discomfort that came with it would have to wait for the sun to rise.

As I headed out of the park, I stopped at a rubbish bin to roll a cigarette. The pervert came out of nowhere to tell me to be careful because somebody had been wanking over me while I was sleeping, then scurried off again. He then turned around and started walking back to me, exposed penis in hand, pleasuring himself furiously and asking me if I liked it.

I was alarmed but not frightened. This wasn't the first disturbing incident I've faced since I found myself in the streets of London, and likely won't be the last. I have received self-defence lessons from my friends in the homeless community and can defend myself enough to buy time and run from a situation.

I grabbed my keys from my pocket and made a fist, slipping them between my fingers, ready to punch him in the eye if necessary. I swung my arm threateningly, shouting at him to "Get the fuck away from me now!" It was enough. He ran away again. He followed at a distance for a brief time, but once I was out of the park and on the street, he disappeared into the darkness and I didn't see him again.

Reflecting on the experience over the course of the day, I wasn't sure what disturbed me more: the incident itself or my reaction to it. I was alarmed; I was disturbed; but for the first time in facing one of the perilous situations that all rough sleepers regularly find themselves, I wasn't particularly frightened nor upset. That was a first, and I was concerned I was viewing the rude awakening as "par for the course" and becoming too hardened to life –a development that would affect not only my writing should I ever return to it, but my basic humanity.

I also had to ponder an issue that all rough sleepers find themselves wrestling with at some point: what to do about it. It is a fairly straightforward decision when you're comfortably ensconced in mainstream life; not so straightforward when you're not. There are issues and ramifications to take into consideration that aren't factors when you're able to return to the safety of your own home, lock the door, and gaze contemplatively at your navel imagining your response to a moral dilemma you will likely never face.

You have a responsibility to get the word out obviously. Other rough sleepers need to know. Forewarned is forearmed. However, that paves the way to vigilante justice that can quickly and violently get out of hand. A lesson I was yet to learn.

Informing the police –anonymously of course to avoid the dangerous reputation as a "grass" whatever the circumstances– is the obvious response. But it opens a problematic can of worms for others sleeping in the park: it is an illegal act. The relationship between the police and the homeless is problematic at best, aggressive and confrontational on a good day. Inviting the patrols such a report would bring also invites conflict and chaos that helps no-one. Even should the police turn a blind eye to their presence, some of your fellow rough sleepers will not react favourably to the increased vigilance –particularly if alcohol, drugs, mental illness, or outstanding arrest warrants are factors. Even my first reaction on waking was "Thank God it's not a cop." By ensuring the safety of your fellow rough sleepers you are opening the door to conflict, violence, and serious injury –including your own, as I was later to discover.

Walking to Trafalgar Square I remembered prior incidents similar not in specifics but in terms of personal safety –one that had occurred just four days previously in front of the National Gallery. I had been rolling a cigarette when a recent addition to the local homeless community demanded some tobacco. I said no. It is a daily exchange on the streets, leading to any number of reactions on a violence scale ranging from 0 to 100. Most times that reaction falls between 0 and 5. His reaction scored a 75 and scared the hell out of me, prompting an anxiety attack. He immediately grew verbally and physically abusive; grabbing my belongings and throwing them while screaming at me to "Fuck off back to my own country!"

Two security guards came by and I asked for help: visibly agitated and not at my most diplomatic. I colourfully asked for him to be removed. They denied the request saying it wasn't their responsibility. They are only there to protect the building. The other man made a lunging movement towards me, said something I don't remember, and I jumped. They all laughed.

Two National Gallery Security Guards laughed at a man suffering an anxiety attack –laughing with the man who caused it.

I went into the Gallery to file a formal written complaint, a process that ended up taking over two and a half hours. During this procedure I was again informed their duty was only to protect the building, not the people. When I asked for a photocopy of the complaint –pointing out I had been a journalist and am in the habit of keeping such documents for my own records, I was denied the request. I was also scoffed at by another Security Guard who recognized me as one of the local homeless community. "Oh come on; no you're not. I see you outside all the time." So I asked for another form and re-copied the complaint for my own records.

The dismissive attitude throughout the process, simply because I had been recognized as one of the local homeless community, added to the humiliation of being laughed at. That night I received a templated email with the barest of modification essentially saying, "Sorry. Please come again." Case closed.

The next day there was a stabbing in Trafalgar Square in front of the National Gallery. (It was an exceptionally bad week, even by homeless standards.) A dispute between two members of the homeless community had grown violently out of hand –100 on the scale. Words were exchanged, punches thrown, a bottle broken and CHUNK! One friend stabbed another in the face. Just another "homeless thing", dismissed and forgotten within days. At least the building was safe. Again, case closed.

Finally, I was forced to reassess the reasons I was sleeping in the park in the first place –for I have been housed. The 'charity approved' accommodation I was forced into accepting was detrimental for a number of reasons: a primary one being the simple fact it is often as dangerous as the streets themselves.

Perhaps because I don't abuse alcohol or drugs myself, I fail to understand the reasoning behind housing alcoholics and drug dependants in the same home. It is, as I have seen first-hand, a recipe for enablement and further descent into addiction –and it can be hazardous, particularly when they are unsupervised.

One unfortunate gentleman with whom I share the house had been so ravaged by his addictions he suffered from psychotic episodes. He has seen ghosts and tried to drive them away by blasting his stereo 24 hours a day, or by leaving all the windows and doors open in the middle of winter. He has had many nights when he's lain in bed screaming at the demons that haunt him. He owned a cat when I first moved in; a lovely, affectionate –and well-cared for– companion. That cat sadly passed away . . . and remained in his room with him for almost two weeks, the smell of its decomposition slowly wafting through the other living quarters. I had smelled something sinister for a number of days but had attributed it to a dietary change in the tenant of Flat Four. Death. Defecation. You don't think to differentiate between the two. They both smell foul.

That same gentleman had been hospitalized on more than one occasion for serious injuries and overdoses in the short time we were co-tenants. He had almost died during one of those visits. He had been waiting, and was eager, to be placed in a rehabilitation facility. He had twice been promised placement within a month, and his joy was heart-wrenching. For reasons unknown neither promise was kept. He was a kind, gentle, giving man when lucid, but a danger to himself and others when not; and he should have been placed in the supervised housing The Connection had previously tried to mislead me into accepting. I feared not so much for an assault by him

–although that is always a possibility– but anything from kitchen appliances to a cigarette lighter was dangerous when he was suffering. He grew thinner and more haggard as his ordeal was allowed to continue.

(He was eventually moved into a rehabilitation facility after the original composition of this piece, and his ordeal finally came to an end. Tragically.)

He was not my only concern. There were five flats in our small two-storey house: five tenants. We were but two. The other three were equally damaged; and had all been placed there by an arrangement between the landlord and Crisis. All but one were chronic alcoholics. It was a hub of enablement, destruction, and chaos. My fears were re-confirmed less than a week after my misadventure in St. James Park had convinced me to give the flat another chance. I had managed a few nights undisturbed sleep indoors, but it was not to last. The dormant drunken violence came storming back with a vengeance.

I woke up around 1:30 a.m. to the sound of shouts coming from the street, loud enough to be heard word for word as they roused me from my slumber.

"Stay the fuck away from me! Fuck you! Show respect or I'll fuckin' cut ya!"
SMASH!

I heard the sound of glass breaking, followed by the high-pitched squeal of a car alarm. The shouts grew louder as he stormed closer.

"Fucking cunts! Fucking respect!"
CRASH!

I heard the razor-sharp sound of a key clattering against the front door. Unsurprisingly he was having difficulties getting his key into the lock, which only made him angrier. He began punching and kicking the door, each thump making me flinch. Eventually the key found its way home, and the door smashed against the wall as he entered.

"And if any of you cunts give me any fucking grief I'll fuckin' cut you too! All of you! Fucking respect! I've had it!"

The hall light came on, the illumination creeping under my door in a two-inch sliver that chilled me. The side table in the hall was thrown to the ground. A wall was thumped; then thumped again. He began to stomp up the stairs to his room on the floor above mine, cursing, raging and pounding the walls with each step. This actually provided a lifeline of hope.

It was, as Fagin croons, time for reviewing the situation.

His next move dictated mine. Would he simply pass out in a few minutes? Would he stay in his room? Or would he continue to rage through the house, looking for the first available person to unleash his anger? Sleep was obviously a lost cause at this point; the decision was whether or not to remain in my room for the night or return to the safety of the streets that this 'charity approved' housing was supposed to be an improvement on.

Again, the metallic click of a key unsuccessfully banging against a lock cut through the night as he tried to enter his room.

"Fuck! Fuck! FU-U-U-UCK!"
   SMASH!
     THUMP!
      "FUCKING FUCK!"

Finally, success. The door smashed against the wall and he entered his room. The swearing and thumping continued for a few minutes until suddenly there was silence.

"Please-pass-out-please-pass-out-please-pass-out-please-pass-out." I lay in bed, shaking, my heart thumping as I prayed for his intoxication to push him into unconsciousness.

"Please-pass-out-please-pass-out-please-pass-out-please-pass-out."

My prayers were denied.

He started screaming again, the verbal and physical violence returning with renewed strength, and he wasn't limiting his rage to the confines of his room. He made his way into the kitchen, the most well-stocked armoury in every home –knives, forks, plates, pots, pans all within easy reach. The time for reviewing the situation was over; it was time to get out.

I had a logistical advantage. He was in the kitchen in the floor above. It made slipping out much easier than it had been in the past; so long as he remained upstairs.

"FUCK!"
  SMASH!
    CLATTER!

That was the cutlery now scattered around the kitchen floor, potential weapons in easy reach. I took advantage of the noise to cover up the sound of my mattress groaning as I slowly slipped out of bed. I didn't dare turn on my light for fear it would shine under the door and reveal my presence, so I slowly, carefully, delicately dressed by the light of the two-inch screen on my cell-phone, making sure to keep the light facing away from the front of my room. It was a long, laborious process complicated by the fact I was shaking so hard. Despite that, I still took the extra time to ensure my socks matched –almost laughing at the absurdity of its sudden importance as a priority.

THUMP!

The kitchen door banged open and he stomped into the upstairs hall, cursing and punching the walls. I froze. If he came downstairs my only avenue of escape was cut off. I closed my eyes, held my breath, and silently prayed he would remain upstairs. "please-Please-PLEASE stay upstairs."

THUMP!
  "FUCKING CUNTS! FUCKING RESPECT! FUCK!"

It was actually the answer I wanted: he had returned to his room. Fully dressed, and with my rucksack having been readied before I went to bed only two hours previously, I grabbed my keys from the wall and gently turned the deadbolt to ensure the 'click' didn't reverberate through the house. I slowly opened the door –grateful the clichéd creaks that accompany all doors in every horror movie ever made was not an issue. Entering the hall, I successfully closed the door in silence, and went to lock it . . .

. . . only to find I couldn't get *my* key into the slot because I was shaking so badly. "You have *GOT* to be kidding me," I thought as I stifled a nervous laugh. "Geez, mate; I feel your pain."

I was eventually successful and moved slowly through the hall to the front door, expertly avoiding the squeaky floorboard whose location I knew from previous escapes. I opened the door with the same care I had used before and made my way outside. I didn't bother closing it behind me. I quickly made my way to the street, turned left, and hurried away. I hadn't breathed once since opening the door to my room.

This was not a rare occurrence. I could ask to be relocated, but under the terms of the lease I was forced to accept –terms that were not disclosed despite my repeated attempts to ascertain them– I am at least one, if not two months in arrears to my landlord. If moved, I will still be responsible for those arrears, as well as the arrears of at least one month I would have to accept in the new lodgings. I would find myself deeper ensnared in a benefits system I fought tooth and nail to avoid, and deeper into a debt I had no need to incur that would keep me trapped in that system even longer.

So I continue to sleep in the streets and parks of London more often than in the "safety" of my 'charity approved' accommodation. Better to be splashed with the sperm of a stranger on a park bench than beaten by a charity-placed housemate in an enclosed space. At least you can run.

For as many have discovered after entering the Tribe of the Homeless, no place is safe. Not the streets, not the security patrolled public areas; not the shelters; and definitely not the housing. You are open to every kind of abuse in every locale from every segment of society. The streets simply provide the best option for the simple fact you are not trapped in an enclosed space. You take the necessary steps to defend yourself and you run like hell. If you're lucky you may receive the assistance of other rough sleepers close by, or your shouts may be heard by an unseen presence within earshot. You learn to trust no-one but a small, close-knit group of friends. But as I soon learned to my horror, you can't even trust them.

For I had befriended a predator.

I Fought the Law

It was not as shocking an epiphany as it should have been. I had long heard the whispers; long seen the signs; long felt something was wrong. Seriously wrong. The truth is I knew. Deep down I knew. I had known for months but couldn't believe it. Didn't want to believe it. Refused to believe it. I made excuses to myself. And to others. I branded the accusations nothing more than rumours, drunken misinterpretations, or malicious lies. I metaphysically stuck my fingers in my ears and placed my hands over my eyes to block out the harsh truth that was screaming in my face.

My figurative 'Partner in Crime', my best friend and protector since my arrival on the streets, had a *real* partner in crime, and their felonies were brutal, vicious, and vile. Drugs, thefts, beatings, sexual assaults. Both ex-convicts with a string of offences and prison stints, they had teamed up after meeting at The Passage, a sister charity of Passage House, and methodically began waging a campaign of terror on the homeless communities in Westminster and Charing Cross. They would volunteer at the food drops and soup kitchens in the surrounding areas and convince the workers and volunteers of their sincerity as reformed convicts who had found salvation in Jesus and wanted to make amends for their past sins. The more religious the charity, the easier it was to pull the wool over their eyes and spoon-feed them lies swallowed with the same blind devotion they surrendered to the Lord. And as the deceitful duo earned the trust of the charities and homeless communities, they slowly began weaving violent new paths of sin through the local streets, alleys, and parks.

They had flown under the radar for months, no-one – myself included– suspecting even the slightest impropriety. Their smiles, their cooperation, and their wide-eyed sincerity fooled everyone. And the charities treasured my street mate for the same self-serving reasons I did: his muscle and his skills as a fighter. He was a valuable asset in keeping order amongst the homeless ranks during food distribution. His physical presence alone was intimidating; his willingness to use physical force at the slightest provocation ensured order and compliance. Few would question him. Even fewer would confront him. He was a veritable godsend to all charities hoping to feed their online brands with photos of happy, disciplined itinerants appreciatively lined up for benevolent tokens of generosity. He offered his voluntary services to many, and they all willingly accepted without question. They all willingly turned a blind eye to the occasional burst of violence and random act of theft. As I did. They all turned a deaf ear to the stories as they started to surface. As I did. He was too good for the brand.

The red flags slowly started to appear. An accusation of rape was directed at his *other* associate. The woman was homeless, a drug addict, and mentally ill. It was waved away as a misinterpretation of his kindness. The charities believed him. I believed him. A few weeks later a homeless man was hospitalized, had two steel plates attached to his skull, after an altercation with my protector who swore with absolute certainty it was only to protect the man's girlfriend from a physical assault. The charities believed him. I believed him.

His *other* partner often took homeless women back to his benefit-paid flat in Hackney –some of them disturbingly young– and the relationships would turn sexual, but there were no further accusations for months so it was easy to lazily brush off as inappropriate but not criminal. The occasional disturbing remark would slip into conversation at Trafalgar Square. The most notable: "I never make the first move. I always show them what's on offer and let them make the first move so they can't charge me with rape," sent chills up a number of spines, including mine, but we all filed it away as crude man-talk. It is easy to deceive yourself when you don't want to believe the truth.

Over a period of months, the stories and accusations increased. Another accusation of sexual assault was casually dismissed. Violent fights were becoming more frequent. They were buying and selling drugs to the hardened addicts of the streets under the guise of drug counselling. They were stealing drugs. They were stealing money. They were stealing from the charities, and the homeless, and laying the fingers of blame on others. I was starting to have doubts myself but as far as the charities were concerned, they were still spotless.

The three of us had been volunteering regularly at one of the street-level charities that visit Charing Cross on a weekly basis to provide food and clothing. They were, and at the time of publication still are, one of the best grassroots organizations serving London. They arrive, distribute the requisite food and clothing, then conduct a walk-around through Leicester Square, Covent Garden and Charing Cross. They take personal interest in the people they help, providing assistance of all kinds and often making themselves available 24 hours a day, seven days a week. They are concrete proof you don't need desks, elegant job titles or bricks and mortar to provide the assistance the homeless need.

During one of those walk-arounds we came across one of the regular clients, a lovely woman –one of the street's earth mothers– known to us all. My friend's partner offered to take her to the Green Room, a woman's shelter in Westminster; and promised to act as her drug counsellor from that day forward. She accepted his offer and arranged to meet with him later that night. She wasn't seen for almost a month and everyone assumed she had been sheltered and was doing well.

Until she returned. And provided a detailed account of the events that transpired after the charity had packed up and returned home. The two gentlemen had returned later that night doing an independent outreach tour after the one conducted with the charity, with meals they had stolen from the charity earlier in the evening. She was not provided the shelter she had been promised earlier. She was provided money to purchase drugs –from the man professing to be a drug and alcohol counsellor. They chatted and she was offered the chance to return to his accommodation in Hackney with the promise of a hot shower. When you're homeless, the promise of a hot shower is far more tempting than food. Food is easy to obtain from the numerous charities that roam the streets; hot showers are not. She accepted.

When she stepped out of the shower her new 'drug counsellor' was standing there, naked, showing her what was on offer and encouraging her to make the first move. She rejected his advances. He persisted. She defended herself and left. My former friend was not a participant in the exchange itself; but was present in the room. Shortly after, the bullying began, encouraging her to leave the area. Others she had known made the effort to come to her defence, only to be met with the intimidating strength of my former friend and protector. He was the brawn in the partnership, being used for his muscle –as he had been by the charities –as he had been by me. And with his brain increasingly addled by the drugs he was taking after being convinced to stop his medication, he was easier to control –and unleash.

She refused to report the incident to the police as she had had prior experience with them in the past and insisted they would do nothing but focus their attentions on her own addictions, not the crime perpetrated against her. The charity owners informed the two gentlemen their voluntary services were no longer required. They gave no indication of pursuing the matter further beyond trying to convince the woman to report the crime. When I suggested reporting it to the police themselves; they disagreed, saying they had dealt with the matter by dismissing the gentlemen who would likely move on, thus solving the problem.

I disagreed.

On 7 November 2019 I reported the incident to the police online through their Twitter account. I provided the details as I knew them and ran through the various rumours and alleged incidents that had occurred over the past few months. Following instructions, I travelled to the police station at Charing Cross where I was questioned about the report I had submitted and sent on my way. I knew my testimony in itself wasn't enough to arrest them but hoped it would lead to an investigation. At least it was on record; at least it was on paper.

I explained my actions to the charity owners who expressed disappointment. They were handling the matter "their way." I was assured not to worry, "the cat was out of the bag now," but they would deal with that, and not to blame myself for the potential complications it would bring them. They were the only people I had informed of my actions and been promised the information would stay with them so I wouldn't get the dangerous reputation of being a "grass" amongst the homeless community.

Word still got out.

On 8 December 2019, I was attacked at Trafalgar Square. I was catching up with another homeless friend who had been out of the area for months on a cycling tour of northern England to visit his family. My former 'partner' was in the vicinity and heard our conversation. I mentioned the book I had recently been contracted to write through a Canadian publisher, and he snapped. He suddenly rushed up to administer a head-butt. I dodged it but took a wild swinging punch to the shoulder that knocked me off my feet.

I leapt up, narrowly avoiding a kick, and ran. He raced after me, shrieking I couldn't hide. I had "played my last joker card." He was going to find me and kill me. He was going to kill my family. He knew people and if he couldn't sort me out, they would. He was going to "tear me apart and show the world how evil I am inside."

Just another 'homeless thing' playing itself out in front of the National Gallery on Trafalgar Square, minutes from The Connection. At least the buildings were safe.

I ran into the new Pret a Manger coffee shop that had recently opened at St. Martin-in-the-Fields screaming for help. Being on a first name basis with the staff, they allowed me to seek sanctuary there, and promised to call the police if he came in and started to cause trouble. I accepted the free coffee they offered, set up my laptop, and contacted the Metropolitan Police on their Twitter account, as I had done before. I also contacted the charity who knew of the situation and the owners abandoned their plans for the day to come to the area.

He entered the store and began pacing up and down the aisles threatening to "tear me apart and show the world how evil I am inside." I was skating on thin ice and needed to walk; he didn't care who my family was, he was going to kill them. Customers started leaving the store. He took a seat behind me shouting I was evil, needed to be torn apart, and he was going to bring me a lot of pain. I was so terrified my bladder was screaming for release, but I was too scared to move from the table. He started pacing the aisles again, brushing by me as he phoned his *other* partner and told him I knew everything and had to be taken down; to round the boys up. I was fucking everybody over and it was time to show me what a real fucking is.

Four police officers arrived and after speaking with the manager on duty, proceeded to the table behind me. The transformation was instantaneous. No longer the screaming, menacing attacker who had sent me fleeing for my life less than a half hour ago; he was suddenly the soft-spoken, charismatic victim. I was the harasser, threatening him and his family for months, and attacking him on more than one occasion. I was crazy and needed to be taken off the streets. He provided the contact details of witnesses who could back up his claims.

Two of the police officers then moved to my table, one staying silent for the entire exchange that followed. My shaking was immediately addressed, and I was asked if I was on drugs. I answered in the negative; and asked if I was sure. I was then told his account did not match the report I had provided online, and he could provide wit-nesses to confirm a history of abusive behaviour on my part. I pointed out the noticeable discrepancy between our sizes and physiques indicating I was in no way a threat to him.

I was then told if I insisted on pressing charges, I would be taken into custody myself. When I asked why I was informed I did not want to add "resisting arrest" to the charges. I was subsequently told to stop coming around the area and creating disturbances. I asked the officer why he was threatening me with arrest; and he replied he wasn't threatening me, he was simply telling me the potential consequences of my decision. I had heard that double-speak before many times, from The Connection and Passage House, and recognized, with alarm, the brick wall of words I was beating my head against.

He then asked what I hoped to achieve from all this. I told him I wanted some assurance I could walk out of the coffee shop and not get beaten up. He told me to stop playing games; that wasn't a real answer. He then asked for my decision, reminding me I would be taken into custody myself if I pressed charges. I asked to wait until the charity owners arrived. He asked why. I answered I was scared, technically a foreigner in this country, unfamiliar with its laws, and wanted their advice. He told me that wasn't possible; the police are busy, and I was wasting their time. Word after word after word; brick after brick after brick.

I opted not to press charges, stating I had felt threatened by the potential arrest my decision could lead to. I was told it was the right decision and told to stay out of the area in future as this incident was now on file. The police left. My former friend remained for some minutes, then also left, brushing past me laughing. I remained in the coffee shop, shaking with fear until the charity owners arrived and after some discussion escorted me out of the area to prevent another attack.

While waiting I received a message on Twitter from the Metropolitan Police asking if I would be willing to complete a short survey about my experience contacting them. I filled it in with the intention of making my displeasure clearly known but the survey itself was not designed to allow for actual criticism. I filled it in as best I could, and the survey ended politely thanking me for my feedback.

And in whichever post-Celestial watering hole they frequent, Orwell and Kafka clinked glasses, toasting their shared foreshadowing of the terrifying absurdity of it all.

The Law Won

On 19 January 2020 I entered the same Pret a Manger where the previous incident had occurred. I was standing in the queue when a hand gripped my arm and a voice said, "I hear you've been spreading tales you little shit. You're fucking dead." I turned to see the brains of the new partnership holding my arm; my former protector standing beside him, grinding his fist into the palm of his other hand and smiling.

During the intervening Christmas season, both men had continued to volunteer for a number of street-level charities; and had continued their harassment. They had also acquired the assistance of other homeless people they had befriended while volunteering. They were informing everyone that not only was I a violent offender; but a thief, and a convicted sex offender, using the newspaper coverage surrounding the *other* Peter Mitchell as proof. Few would actually read the stories themselves, just the headlines. Some people believed them; some didn't.

A major theft had also occurred at The Soup Kitchen associated with the American International Church on

Tottenham Court Road where my former friend was volunteering. He informed them I was the person behind the crime and should be reported to the police, as well as denied access to their services. They had enough doubts about my physical strength to question my ability to have conducted the burglary; and continued to allow me access to their meals and services. Other charities were not so benevolent, and I found myself turned away from their food drops and Christmas events. These were worrying developments, but no specific threats were made against me. Until I found myself literally in his grip in the queue at Pret a Manger.

He shoved me away, stood back and pointed, shouting for the entire coffee shop to hear: "THIS MAN IS A PAEDOPHILE! He is not allowed back to Canada because he rapes children! And he is now raping children here!"

He pulled out his Smart Phone and announced the proof could be found with an online search; and started reading newspaper headlines referring to the *other* Peter Mitchell, clearly identifying him as a paedophile. He raised his phone to show one of those headlines prominently displayed, and slowly turned to give all eyes in the immediate vicinity the chance to read it.

He went on to shout I was also a violent drug addict who beats up members of the homeless community; and a thief, stealing from the good charities that try to help. He identified himself as a Drug and Alcohol Counsellor –brandishing one of the business cards he had had printed– and was there with his associate to take me to

the police station at Charing Cross to stop me from raping people's children. He didn't want to alarm anyone;
but stated they may need assistance if I grew violent.

Every pair of eyes in the store looked at me as I began
shaking uncontrollably. He seized on that to loudly pro-
claim I was on drugs right now and could turn violent at
any time. A few customers hurriedly left the store. The
young woman on the till, frightened, asked me to please
leave. I made a few slow steps toward the exit when my
former friend lunged. I ran out of the shop screaming at
the top of my lungs. He came after me. I raced down the
street to the Charing Cross police station a block away,
screaming for help as he pursued me.

I ran screaming into the station. The woman at the
desk immediately told me to leave. I caught my breath,
steadied myself as best I could, and gaspingly informed
her two men were after me, were trying to kill me, and
were standing outside the station waiting for me.

She told me I had to use the online form to report a
crime.

I shouted, "Are you fucking kidding me?" She said I
was being verbally abusive to her and if I didn't leave immediately, she would have me escorted out. She picked
up the phone next to her and looked at me, her fingers
poised over the dial pad.

I left the station and saw both men at the end of the
street. I phoned the charity in a state of crying hysteria,
and they immediately offered to drive down to assist. For
the next hour I stood in front of the Charing Cross police
station frozen in terror while the two men inspiring that

fear stood within eyesight; making threatening comments, laughing, and engaging with other members of the homeless community who were waiting for another charity's food drop –showing them the display on the Smart Phone and pointing at me.

When the charity owners arrived, we entered the station and the woman on the desk agreed to have an officer speak with us. After a small wait, one of the owners and I were invited into an office to explain the situation. He did most of the talking for which I was tearfully grateful. At first.

He introduced himself and his charity, understandably highlighting the work they did and the genuine trust they had earned from the local homeless community, including myself. He was correct on all accounts. I was, and remain, in complete agreement; and didn't hesitate to make that fact known. He made reference to a 'Sleep Out' event they were organizing to raise funds and awareness; and though I was quietly starting to wish we could move on and address the matter at hand, didn't begrudge him the opportunity to use the situation to promote their upcoming endeavours.

The conversation turned to the issues that had brought us there: the assault of the woman I had reported; and the subsequent threats and attacks that included other cases of harassment I didn't report to the police, as the immediate threat to my life was not present on those occasions. All too quickly I found myself relegated to the condescending stereotype I had experienced with previous charities: the naughty child who doesn't understand the complexities of the adult world and needs the charities to survive; and do all their thinking –and talking– for them.

I had reported the assaults, both on the woman and myself seemingly without understanding how complex these matters are, and the difficulties it presented to the police. The charity owner, of course, did. He was obsequiously sympathetic to the police and the good work they do. He had tried to offer advice and guidance, but I still didn't understand how complicated these matters are. (Personally, I don't see much complexity in trying to prevent sexual and physical assaults –particularly when the threat of physical assault against myself is imminent– but what do I know? I'm only homeless.)

He also understood while incidents like these "are unfortunate," he knew there was little the police could do. I took that opportunity to disagree. My former friend's previous convictions include assaults against the police. Over the past year he had been tried, convicted, and served a three-month prison term for one such assault. I had supported him throughout and was familiar with the evidence that had been used in the prosecution. I began listing the possibilities I thought may be useful to my immediate predicament.

I asked about the Closed-Circuit Television cameras in the coffee shop and surrounding vicinity, as they had provided crucial evidence in my former friend's previous police assault. The officer informed me CCTV cameras aren't useful because they don't have sound. The charity owner nodded his agreement.

I asked about witnesses: the staff and customers of the coffee shop where these events had transpired. I was subsequently told personal witness testimony is ineffective and unreliable. The charity owner continued to nod fawningly.

I asked about the possibility of a restraining order. The charity owner spoke up at that point informing me they were expensive and not worth the money because they don't really work; his new friend the police officer nodding his agreement in turn.

I asked if the police could at least speak to the gentlemen themselves and tell them to back off. They were standing outside the station while we were having this meeting. Again, no. The police are not there to act as my own personal security force. Nods all round.

I pointed out the discrepancy between these being valid tools used in cases of assault against the police themselves, yet seemingly invalid when assaults are made against the homeless. I was again informed it was more complicated than I realized, and he could try to explain but I wouldn't understand.

I was told to stop coming into London –except of course to volunteer with the charity, apparently my only valid reason for being there. I mentioned I feared the two men would track me down to where I had been housed and attack me there. I was told I was being silly and over-reacting. That would not happen.

Word after word after word. Brick after brick after brick. Nod after nod after nod. I recognized the familiar wall I was banging my head against and realized I would not make any progress in my attempts to prevent being physically attacked.

My heart sank as the conversation turned back to the 'Sleep Out' event being organized and the importance of building bridges between the police and the homeless through these charity events. The officer agreed to provide details of the person to contact to discuss how the police could assist with the event. It proved a wonderful networking opportunity for both; just not for the homeless community they were building bridges to help – particularly those who had been sexually assaulted or were in current danger of physical violence. We are just "unfortunate."

As the meeting drew to a close, I grudgingly agreed to not request action be brought against the men who were threatening my life, stressing I was unhappy with the outcome but felt I had no other choice. He assured me he would add my concerns to his report. He didn't.

We left the police station, passing the charity food-drop currently in operation beside it –being assisted by the two upstanding reformed Christians who were still a threat to my life. I was disgusted, livid, and still frightened. I returned to my flat and turned my phone off, too angry to discuss the events with anyone until I had the opportunity to think them through. I did not want to be disturbed by anyone.

Four days later I discovered I was on the Missing Person list.

The charity owners had been unable to contact me, so contacted a family member asking him to report my worrying absence. I immediately phoned the Detective from the Missing Persons Unit assigned to my case and the matter was easily resolved. I had actually done what I had been instructed and stayed home. I had simply turned off my phone, an understandable reaction in her opinion. The police investigating my "disappearance" had not even bothered to knock on my front door.

We discussed the circumstances surrounding my "disappearance," and she expressed surprise at my frustration because on the previous incident reports it stated I was satisfied with the outcomes. I clarified I had not been satisfied in the slightest and had made that perfectly clear at the time. I had wanted my dissatisfaction and the belief I had felt bullied into agreement clearly specified on the reports. She believed me and promised to have my concerns addressed. She advised me to keep pressing for charges to be laid, and to try to contact higher ranking police officers than the ones I had been dealing with. She promised to do what she could as well.

She kept those promises. On 27 January 2020 I received an email from the officer I had met at the Charing Cross Police Station, asking me if I would still like to give a statement and progress the incident to the stage of having the suspect arrested. I responded in the affirmative and also requested the procedures required to file a formal complaint. Not receiving a response, I sent a follow-up email on 30 January asking for an appointment. I sent a third email on 31 January asking for a response. On 1

February he apologized for the delay stating he had been out of the office all week; and arranged an interview at the Charing Cross Police Station at 9 a.m. on 6 February.

I arrived. It was the same desk officer I had encountered before and she greeted me with, "You again. What do you want?"

I informed her I had an appointment with the officer I had spoken to previously. She said she would call upstairs and let him know. An hour and a half later he had not arrived. I twice asked her to remind him I was waiting, and she promised to do so. After another fifteen minutes I concluded he would not be coming down to speak with me. I told the officer on the desk I was leaving, and she said she would inform him of my decision.

I made my way to the coffee shop where I could access their free wi-fi connection and checked my emails for the first time that day. There was a communication dated the night before informing me he was needed elsewhere on Public Order duties and cancelling the appointment. He offered to take my statement over the phone or to reschedule our meeting for 7 February between 10 and 12. I wanted to handle the matter in person and agreed to return for the time he requested.

I returned before 9:45 the next morning, and the same desk officer promised to inform him of my arrival. I waited over *three hours* and he again did not appear. As before, I asked for him to be reminded of my presence and received the same assurance she would let him know. Realizing the futility of another wasted journey, I again told the desk officer I could not wait any longer and left.

I returned to the same coffee shop and on accessing the internet found an email sent at 11:20. He stated he understood I was at the Charing Cross Station, but he was based at the West End Central Station –a claim that stood in stark contrast to the station listed on all his online communications. He had offered to come to Charing Cross for 12:30. The time was now well past 2:00. He also claimed he did not start his shift until 11:00 –despite asking for a meeting at 10:00. I grew fed up with the costly and time-wasting run-around I was getting and gave up all hope of assistance from the Metropolitan Police.

I immediately had more pressing concerns.

For despite the condescending admonitions from the police officer and the charity owner my concerns were "silly," they proved valid. My former friend had followed me to Croydon, was staying in the Wellington Hostel on Lansdowne Road, was arranging to have a charity house him in the area, and spreading the same slanderous accusations about my paedophilia convictions to the local homeless community and business owners.

Our paths unexpectedly crossed the morning after my second aborted attempt to meet with the officer at Charing Cross station. He shouted "Ha," and proceeded to chase me down the street, again screaming, "I'm going to tear you apart and show the world how evil you are inside," and "You've played your last Joker card!" I ran for my life, jumping on the first available bus to escape. He continued the chase and for a few terrifying moments I feared he would catch up at one of the subsequent stops. Those fears ultimately proved groundless, and I spent the remainder of the day, riding buses throughout London before returning to my flat late that night, terrified he had managed to find that location and be waiting for me.

I spent the next few days in a permanent state of dread he would appear at my 'charity approved' home. I was also concerned about the easy access to my room. The glass door leading from my room into the back yard has no lock. Anyone can enter. Despite numerous requests to the landlord to have one installed, it still remained an easy point of access fifteen months after I had been forced into tenancy. I was also terrified he would be placed in my accommodation through the charities assisting him, for a room had been available for a number of weeks. Every phone call and every knock at the door made me jump with fright.

I was just as fearful of leaving, limiting my actions to odd times of the day and night, and taking long circuitous routes to avoid being followed. The enemy you can't see is far more unnerving than the enemy you can. At least when you see him, you know which direction to run. When he is hovering, lurking, skulking –unseen in the periphery– every step you take could lead to a surprise, possibly fatal encounter. I saw him numerous times over the following month but managed to slip away unseen. My attempts at stealth ultimately proved futile, as I knew they would.

On 5 March 2020 I was standing at the bus stop on Wellesley Road at 4:15 a.m. to catch a bus into London. The street was deserted, but I was still caught by surprise when I suddenly heard someone shout, "You're that fucking paedo," behind me.

It was one of the local homeless community. He shouted, "Fucking pervert," and moved to head-butt me. I countered with a head-butt of my own and scored a direct hit; my forehead smashing into his mouth, splashing blood on both our faces. I rammed his groin with my knee, and as he started to crumple, kicked his feet out from under him and shoved him to the ground. I kicked him in the stomach three times. As he grabbed for his mobile phone gasping "Police," and "Paedo", I kicked it out of his hand, watched it smash into the brick wall a few feet away and land on the ground. I jumped to where it lay and proceeded to stomp on it repeatedly, shattering it to ensure it remained unquestionably inoperable.

I redirected my attention back to my accuser. He lay on his side, holding his stomach and repeating, "Fucking paedo," as best he could through the blood streaming out of his mouth. My fury immediately changed to mortification at what I had just done. I had used physical force to defend myself on three separate occasions since becoming homeless, but never with such violence. On every previous occasion I had surprise on my side, and an unexpected head-butt or quick punch in the mouth was enough to buy me enough time to run. I wasn't sure of the exact criteria for justifiable force was in relation to self-defence, but I was fairly certain I had surpassed them.

I was also relieved I had switched jackets that morning and had failed to transfer the scissors I had been keeping in its pocket in lieu of the broken bottle neck I had been taught to have readily available "just in case." I had pointedly been carrying them for over a month as my efforts to obtain police assistance proved increasingly futile. I had chastised myself for the oversight when I initially discovered their absence barely twenty minutes prior to this incident. All I felt now was chilling relief. Go for the throat indeed.

I said, "Shit! Are you okay?"

He kept repeating "Fucking paedo," as he slowly started to pick himself up.

I watched him stagger to his feet for a few moments, then turned and ran. I returned to my flat, stuffed a few belongings in my rucksack, and kept running. With no idea what to do, where to go, or who to turn to; I left London, and the worsening nightmare my dream had become.

The Unwritten End

Inevitably I had to return. For I had been housed. My homelessness had been successfully resolved to the satisfaction of the charities; my "happy ending" achieved. I was locked into a lease that had left me a month in arrears; in conditions neither safe nor stable; dependent on benefits I did not need when I first turned to the charities for help. When all was said and done and the paperwork completed, I was left in possession of an over-priced, over-glorified wardrobe to store my clothes and few possessions while I continued to sleep in the relative safety of the streets. I did not want to risk losing the storage space, so I eventually returned.

Some months had passed, but little had changed. I no longer appeared to be under the threat of a random vigilante attack, but my former friend and current adversary was still lurking, having been successfully housed in the area. I spied him a few more times; and was able to slip away unnoticed before stumbling into his sight.

Inevitably our paths crossed. I was rolling a cigarette on a rubbish bin on Wellesley Road when he unexpectedly came around a corner in his now familiar rage. Punching and kicking the air as he stormed, his rants and shouts were interspersed with the singing of random song lyrics. His appearance was so sudden I hadn't had time to race out of view, and his eyes locked on mine.

Without recognition.

He looked right through me and passed me by, continuing his song-filled tirade down the street. A little under three weeks later our paths crossed again. He was again raging, rambling, and singing random song lyrics with little coherence I could discern. I pointedly moved into his view and, terrified, uttered a friendly "Hey," as he neared. He looked at me, again without recognition, and continued on his way.

I still feared him. I still hated him. But surprisingly, my heart broke for him.

For that man had been a genuine friend, a 'Partner in Crime' who had watched my back, saved my life, and added his skill set to mine so together we had a fighting chance at survival. I was the brains; he was the brawn. But it wasn't enough. We both suffered our individual slings and arrows of outrageous fortune until the friendship shattered. We both refused to play the games we knew were not in our best interests, and we had both paid the price. His story will always remain more tragic than mine.

Our homeless situations should have been quick fixes yet proved to be anything but. For the streets are vicious, the charities more so. And like so many others we had been broken by the process, and forced unnecessarily into a relentless cycle of bureaucracy, zealotry and abuse that never ends; the "successful resolutions" providing a shaky, porous foundation too easily upended by the actions of others, intentional or not. We were now two broken husks of the men we had once been –neutered, neutralized, and hobbling to our inevitable, pre-ordained fates. Fates decreed not by God; but by the good Christian charities that serve in his name. You can't fight fate; you can't fight the charities. The endings to both our homeless odysseys had been written for us. We had no choice but to accept them.

Except for one small glimmer of hope.

Big Bird had done his job well.

My former media employers knew it; and had allowed me to bumble through a moderately successful career in journalism. My family knew it, and had supported me in my spontaneous, ill-thought out pursuit of my writing dreams. The charities knew it; and were eager to exploit it –free of charge– to promote themselves and their cause, while I remained stubbornly unemployed. And when I refused, they retaliated –assuring me no-one would believe me because I was homeless.

It was time to put Big Bird's lessons to good use. To reveal my experiences within the system. To share my side of the story, my "unofficial" interpretations of the conversations and events not reflected in the "official" paperwork. To encourage others to finally look behind the curtain; and re-write the endings the charities have been dictating in the decades since my great, great grandfather received his now questionable knighthood.

It was time to stand and be heard. To encourage others to take the same stand, and demand their stories be given the spotlight. For myself. For my friend. For the women sexually assaulted by a man who at the time of publication has still not been brought to account, and still volunteers for charities in the streets of London. And for the thousands of others, past and present, that have found themselves broken behind closed charity doors. Theirs are the stories that need to be heard.

So I picked up a pen . . .

My Name is Peter Mitchell

It's the faces that haunt you, more than the actions themselves. The faces that slip into your dreams unannounced, jolting you awake in the middle of the night drenched in the clammy sweat of fear. The faces that randomly enter your thoughts over the course of the day when your memory is nudged by a chance encounter, a random exchange on the street, or a newspaper headline. The faces that hover unseen around you, waiting for that precise moment to leap into view and remind you of the horrors they inflicted. The terror they inspired. The pain they wreaked.

It's the faces –the eyes –Nature's own windows to the soul– that plant themselves deep in your memory, their roots stretching like tentacles through your psyche, embedding themselves permanently into your being; never to be uprooted, never to be excavated, never to be ploughed. It's the eyes that come swimming into view when the memories resurface; the eyes that lock you in their gaze with their timeless intensity; the eyes that condemn you with trauma's damnation. The eyes stay with you forever.

The unhinged rage in the eyes of your former best friend as he screams, "I'm going to tear you apart and show the world how evil you are inside," as he chases you down a public street to administer a bone-breaking, blood-spattered beating.

The arrogant confidence in the eyes of the police officer as he warns, "You don't want to add resisting arrest to your charges," after your attempts to seek protection, not only for yourself but for a friend who had been sexually assaulted, see you threatened with arrest yourself for making false accusations and disturbing the peace.

The terror in the eyes of the stranger you have just beaten with a viciousness greater than self-defence requires after he assaulted you in the street with the erroneous certainty you are a paedophile.

The deranged carnality in the eyes of the pervert when you awaken to find him stroking his penis over your sleeping face.

The soul-destroying humiliation in the eyes of the friend as he screams when you decline his lonely, confused, drug-addled sexual advances –two months before his death from an overdose.

The drunken incomprehension in the bloodshot eyes of your housemate when his beloved cat is removed after the foul stench of decomposition alerted others two weeks after its death.

The victorious malice in the eyes of your case worker when she sees you break after she declares, "Nobody's going to believe you anyway, because you're homeless." Those are the eyes that haunt my dreams the most.

These are the eyes –the faces– the charities don't want you to see. The stories they don't want you to hear. The narratives they want to stay buried. These are the true faces of homelessness that belie the faux-reality presented to the public in endless fund-raising campaigns through smiling charity-selected, charity-tailored, charity-groomed "pets" advertising the successful resolutions the charities promote. These are the faces the public needs to see; the voices the public needs to hear.

Scooby Doo was right. My mother was right. There are no ghosts in this world. There are no phantasmal apparitions floating through haunted houses waiting to shimmer into view and shriek "Boo!" There are no wraiths hiding in the shadows waiting to materialize and seek revenge for crimes long forgotten in the dusty annals of history. There are no spectral messengers twiddling their ectoplasmic thumbs in the mystical aether, waiting for the next séance to deliver their otherworldly missives. There are no ghosts. They are figments of the imagination.

There are no ghosts, but there are demons. Demons that live within us all. Demons of varying sizes, of varying strengths, of varying malevolence. Some can be tamed; others refuse control. Some are relatively inconsequential; others vent their consequences with volcanic rage; the fallout creating tragic, sometimes fatal devastation. They are our fears, our uncertainties, our weaknesses, our addictions. They slumber deep within the consciousness for days, weeks, even years, benign in their dormancy. But they sleep softly, ever alert for the trigger, the outside call to awaken them. And when the call sounds, they are rested and eager to play.

There are demons. And there are monsters. The monsters surround us. In our homes. In our offices. Our streets and our parks. They queue in the food-lines. They sleep in the shelters. They volunteer within the charities themselves. They smile, they lurk, they wait, they hunt – often staring right at us but remaining unseen. They smile. They watch. They listen. They sniff. Sniffing for weakness; sniffing for fear; sniffing for demons; sniffing for prey. When they catch their coveted scent they smile, they circle, they study, they probe –looking for the sleeping demons to awaken them. To unleash them. To exploit them. To wallow in their chaos and feed upon it. In unleashing our demons, the monsters create the eyes, the faces, the nightmares and the memories that haunt us for the rest of our lives.

I was prepared for the ghosts. I was prepared for the demons. I wasn't prepared for the monsters.

My name is Peter Mitchell. Peter Christian Mitchell to be precise, for reasons I hope my account makes clear.

My name is Peter Mitchell, and these are the ghosts that haunt me.

Afterword

As a reader your knee-jerk reaction may be to find a local homeless shelter or charity and make a donation.

Don't.

Please don't.

No matter how sincere your intention, it would be a slap in the face not only to my own suffering, but to the misery of thousands over the decades. There is nothing exceptional in my story. Not one of my experiences is unique. If anything, my suffering pales in comparison to the trauma others have borne from the distant past to the present day.

The charities have been controlling the narrative surrounding poverty and homelessness for far too long. John Kirk was a master at it, earning a knighthood for his powers of spin and persuasion. At the same time he was responsible for the suffering of thousands; needlessly tearing families apart and fanatically sending their children to the colonies to spread God's Army and build the British Empire –bamboozling the public with a non-stop public relations campaign highlighting the benefits to these impoverished waifs, and raising thousands of pounds to send more.

All too often these children were sent into lives of indentured servitude and endured horrific violence and sexual abuse –sometimes even killed. Their letters home often written for them, or in the presence of their masters, preventing the truth from getting out. When the reality slowly started to emerge, the charities responded with renewed force –insinuating any who dared question them were the true villains. Almost a century later the governments of England, Australia and Canada issued formal apologies to the families who had been unnecessarily torn apart and the lives destroyed by the aggressive zeal of my great, great grandfather and others empowered by their own self-righteousness, and drunk with the authority of their "cause." The Home Child Scandal should have been the red flag to alert people to the dangers of blind faith in the charity system. Sadly, that epiphany failed to materialize. Even sadder, it was not the only red flag.

I came to England thinking John Kirk was a family hero. After falling victim to the lies, abuse and corruption in the system he helped establish, I consider him the family's greatest shame. My experiences opened my eyes. Please let those experiences open yours.

By donating in blind faith, you are potentially funding abuse, enabling addictions, supporting crime, and extending suffering. And your contributions are not necessarily providing direct support to the people who most need them. They may be paying the salaries of employees whose jobs have little, if any direct influence on the impoverished you are hoping to assist. You may be funding studies –the same studies that have been conducted for decades– to present reports – the same reports that have been presented for decades– that invariably blame the government and the parents –and demand more money to fight these twin "evils." You may be sponsoring "Sleep Out" events that unwittingly insult the hard-core homeless with the same boorish ignorance as wearing blackface to fight racism or sporting a dress to promote understanding of transgender rights. You may be subsidising creative ventures that pluck carefully selected representatives off the streets, shine a spotlight on their "charity edited" plights, then leave them perched on the same abyss they were found on, with no practical help provided.

Far too many have fallen into that abyss, and permanently succumbed to their addictions, their illnesses, their criminal natures, their despair. Far too many have taken their own lives. You are conceivably perpetuating problems rather than providing solutions.

The system is not broken so much as it is porous with abuse. It has been abused for decades, much like the victims forced into it; much like the victims who can't escape. It needs change. Radical change. It needs greater transparency, independent regulation, stronger legislation, and stricter punishments for corruptions and abuses. It needs modification to better support people striving for true independence –not 'charity approved' co-dependence that can be pulled away at a moment's notice with a sanction or at Her Majesty's –or charity's–

displeasure. You don't need a career in business journalism to know that the best customer is a repeat customer.

As more corporations, local businesses and community leaders are answering the call and using their own pre-existing resources to establish distribution networks for food and clothing, and offering practical advice and assistance, they are doing the charities' work more efficiently, cost effectively –and free of the charity "agendas" that corrupt the process. The charities, in short, are an increasingly unnecessary middleman. They need to be removed from the narrative; removed from the benefits system; removed from the equation altogether. You don't need charity status to feed a hungry woman. You don't need charity status to clothe a destitute man. They have had almost 200 years to, in Crisis' words, "end homelessness" and they have failed miserably. The causes remain the same; the issues remain the same. John Kirk's solutions remain the same. And his solutions are not working.

Please *don't* support the charity coffers. To be crass, support mine. Support the man, not the cause. Buy the book. Buy multiple copies. And use it to spread the word; not the Gospel truth -the *real* truth.

For the writing of this book is motivated in part by a desire to use my occupational skills to finally escape this nightmare I unwittingly joined. Skills salaried charity employees were willing to exploit for their own self-promotion with no intention of payment, while preventing me from obtaining the employment I needed to avoid the nightmare altogether.

Donate this book to the rough sleepers that adorn your commute to inspire them to share their own tales of abuse with the traditional media and elected officials, free of charity influence and unhindered by charity-provoked fear. Provide them the hope people *will* listen, *will* believe them, and *will* take action. Theirs are the stories that need to be heard. Seek them out. Share them. Support them.

Provide copies of this book to the traditional media outlets who know these stories exist, but find their attempts to uncover them obstructed by the same charities that condemn them for trying to peddle poverty porn in their attempts to uncover the truth. The same charities that take offence when their repetitive self-endorsing media releases are ignored. Remind the media these stories exist, and encourage them to keep looking, keep digging, keep the scrutiny alive.

Share this book with your elected officials, your business owners, and your community leaders. Remind them they can follow the example set by others and take a larger role in the issues surrounding poverty and homelessness. Encourage them to take control of the machinery the charities have been operating unchecked for far too long and return them to their rightful place as a single cog in the machine –easily controlled and easily replaced. It was an investigation into Corporate Social Responsibility that provided the initial spark that led me down this path of woe. Let this path of woe provide the spark that encourages local leaders to follow the path others have already forged.

Use this book to educate others. Deliver copies to your local libraries and educational institutions: the true think tanks –independent study facilities whose academic professionals have no vested interest in the outcome of their findings. Help this book open more eyes to the abuse and corruption; encourage others to ask questions, demand answers, demand results, demand change. Real change. Lasting change. Put an end to the distracting noise generated by the charity public relations machine. End the donations given in blind faith. End the lies and half-truths. End the corruption and abuse. End the suffering. End the waste.

Please, don't feed the brands.

Feed a homeless person instead.

Thank you.

ABOUT THE AUTHOR

London born, Canadian raised Peter Mitchell was bumbling his way through a moderately successful career in business journalism when an investigation into a story on Corporate Social Responsibility inspired him to look beyond profit margins and PR into the very real problems faced by society. This inspiration prompted him to dip his toes into a self-confessed Sanity/Vanity project of a biography of his great, great grandfather, Sir John Kirk.

As Secretary of The Ragged School Union, John championed the causes of children, the disabled, and the working poor in Victorian-era London. His influence extended beyond the city limits, and his life proved more interesting than previous biographies revealed. Dust-buried references have surfaced in the most obscure locales, showing the consequences—both good and bad—to the ragged and crippled children John Kirk devoted his life to help.

In 2017, Peter returned to London to complete his research and begin the writing of "A Knight in the Slums." The past was ready to be mined, and the future was assured. The present, however, took an unpredictable -and darkly ironic—turn.

A series of unfortunate events transpired, creating a perfect storm of calamities leaving Peter penniless and sleeping rough. He had unwittingly fallen victim to the same societal ailments John Kirk fought. That nightmare inadvertently provided him with an inside look into the current workings of these same systems put in place by his great, great grandfather, and others like him, put in place over a century ago. That experience frightened him more than the horrors of homelessness itself.

Armed with the scars of this unexpected, but disturbingly relevant, knowledge Peter continues to work on "A Knight in the Slums" with renewed insight. John Kirk created solutions over 100 years ago that are still in play today. Times have changed; yet the solutions have stagnated, and proven to not be solutions, but mechanisms that perpetuate the cycle of poverty: a Hell's Carousel funded by well-meant individuals and institutions blinded by the brand of "charity." New systems need to be developed; new solutions need to be found.